THE MARKETISATION OF ENGLISH HIGHER EDUCATION

Great Debates in Higher Education is a series of short, accessible books addressing key challenges to and issues in Higher Education, on a national and international level. These books are research informed but debate driven. They are intended to be relevant to a broad spectrum of researchers, students and administrators in higher education and are designed to help us unpick and assess the state of higher education systems, policies, and social and economic impacts.

Published titles:

Teaching Excellence in Higher Education: Challenges, Changes and the Teaching Excellence Framework
Edited by Amanda French and Matt O'Leary

British Universities in the Brexit Moment: Political, Economic and Cultural Implications
Mike Finn

Sexual Violence on Campus: Power-conscious Approaches to Awareness, Prevention, and Response
Chris Linder

Higher Education, Access and Funding: The UK in International Perspective
Edited by Sheila Riddell, Sarah Minty, Elisabet Weedon and Susan Whittaker

Evaluating Scholarship and Research Impact: History, Practices, and Policy Development
Jeffrey W. Alstete, Nicholas J. Beutell and John P. Meyer

Forthcoming titles:

Access to Success and Social Mobility through Higher Education: A Curate's Egg?
Edited by Stuart Billingham

Cultural Journeys in Higher Education: Student Voices and Narratives
Jan Bamford and Lucy Pollard

Refugees in Higher Education: Debate, Discourse and Practice
Jacqueline Stevenson and Sally Baker

Radicalisation and Counter-radicalisation in Higher Education
Catherine McGlynn and Shaun McDaid

THE MARKETISATION OF ENGLISH HIGHER EDUCATION

A Policy Analysis of a Risk-based System

BY

COLIN McCAIG
Sheffield Hallam University, UK

United Kingdom – North America – Japan
India – Malaysia – China

Emerald Publishing Limited
Howard House, Wagon Lane, Bingley BD16 1WA, UK

First edition 2018

Copyright © 2018 Emerald Publishing Limited

Reprints and permissions service
Contact: permissions@emeraldinsight.com

No part of this book may be reproduced, stored in a retrieval system, transmitted in any form or by any means electronic, mechanical, photocopying, recording or otherwise without either the prior written permission of the publisher or a licence permitting restricted copying issued in the UK by The Copyright Licensing Agency and in the USA by The Copyright Clearance Center. Any opinions expressed in the chapters are those of the authors. Whilst Emerald makes every effort to ensure the quality and accuracy of its content, Emerald makes no representation implied or otherwise, as to the chapters' suitability and application and disclaims any warranties, express or implied, to their use.

British Library Cataloguing in Publication Data
A catalogue record for this book is available from the British Library

ISBN: 978-1-78743-857-6 (Print)
ISBN: 978-1-78743-856-9 (Online)
ISBN: 978-1-78743-994-8 (Epub)

Printed and bound by CPI Group (UK) Ltd, Croydon, CR0 4YY

ISOQAR certified Management System, awarded to Emerald for adherence to Environmental standard ISO 14001:2004.

Certificate Number 1985
ISO 14001

INVESTOR IN PEOPLE

CONTENTS

List of Tables vii

Introduction: The Marketisation of English Higher Education   1

1. The Genesis of Market Reforms: Efficiency, Accountability and the Celebration of Diversity   25

2. From Diversity to Differentiation: The Coming of the Market   57

3. The Higher Education and Research Act 2017: The Road to Risk and Exit   95

4. Continuity and Discontinuity on the Road to Risk and Exit: Stages of Marketisation in Comparative Policy Analysis   125

Bibliography   165

Index   179

LIST OF TABLES

Introduction

Table I.1.	The Cumulative Effect of Marketisation Discourse.	5

Chapter 1

Table 1.1.	Stage Analysis Table 'Accountability and Efficiency'.	52
Table 1.2.	Stage Analysis Table 'Diversity as a Good'.	54

Chapter 2

Table 2.1.	Stage Analysis Table 'Diversity to Differentiation'.	90
Table 2.2.	Stage Analysis Table 'Competitive Differentiation'.	92

Chapter 3

Table 3.1.	Stage Analysis Table 'Risk and Exit'.	122

Chapter 4

Table 4.1.	Centralisation versus Autonomy.	146
Table 4.2.	Efficiency in Public Services/Individual Return on Investment.	148
Table 4.3.	Funding Mode.	149
Table 4.4.	New Sources of Income.	150
Table 4.5.	Human Capital.	151
Table 4.6.	Widening Participation: Diversity as a Good.	152

Table 4.7.	Quality.	155
Table 4.8.	Tuition Fees.	156
Table 4.9.	Opening Up the Market and Choice for Applicants.	157

INTRODUCTION: THE MARKETISATION OF ENGLISH HIGHER EDUCATION

This book traces the long development of a recognisably marketised higher education (HE) system in England over a 30-year period from the mid-1980s and identifies five distinct stages of market reforms culminating in the Higher Education and Research Act (HERA) (HMSO, 2017) which introduced the risk of institutional exit (DBIS, 2015, 2016) to the already competitive market system established by earlier policy change (DBIS, 2011; DfES, 2003; HM Government, 2004). The HERA effectively shifts the risks of institutional failure onto students by presenting them with ever more applicant choice information and encouraging them to use their consumer behaviour to oblige weaker providers either to lower tuition fees or to lose market share to (newly encouraged) competitors. The new Office for Students (OfS) would regulate the system through the application of risk, concentrating its oversight mainly on those institutions that perform poorly against a range of monitoring data, including those relating to teaching quality. The OfS would no longer prop up (through student number allocations or cash) those institutions that failed in this newly competitive environment, and it would overtly encourage new providers to replace them – by taking their market share – or to create additional supply. Either or both of these mechanisms are assumed by policymakers to create a further fee differential by reducing the average tuition fee charged by providers that are not deemed to be the best. This represents a marked departure from previous attempts to introduce market dynamism into the sector and places the English HE system at the forefront of marketisation. This book, which traces the development of policy over a 30-year period, can therefore act as a 'how-to' guide or a warning of things to come in comparative analysis.

The various policy stages analysed in the following chapters often employ discourses apparent in previous stages of rationalisation of policy (albeit sometimes in other guises) and it is the purpose of this book to focus mainly on the arguments thus employed. They can perhaps be best understood as building blocks contributing to the extant edifice of marketisation presented here. In order to set policy reforms in their appropriate context, the book addresses the following set of questions: to what extent has there been a continuity of policy from the encouragement of public expenditure efficiencies and accountability in the 1980s to the emphasis on competition and risk in 2017? Was there an intention among policymakers that the system would have to go through incremental stages of marketisation to reach the 2017 position? (In other words, was it designedly cumulative, as part of a deliberate and phased policy of neoliberalisation of the sector?) Alternatively, has marketisation developed in response to factors beyond the control of policymakers, with government essentially reactive to factors out of its control? What role has the introduction of tuition fees paid by students (and subsequent increases) played in the development of marketisation in the English context? What, if anything, does the English case tell us about the nature of neoliberalism or indeed the future trajectories of other national systems in the process of marketising and differentiating their institutions, such as the German Excellence Initiative? (Knie & Simon, 2018).

STRUCTURE OF THE BOOK

This account is based on a policy discourse analysis (PDA) of a dozen policy statements over a 30-year period. These are variously government-sponsored reviews, funding council reports and position papers, Green and White Papers and Acts of Parliament that have been used to argue for the introduction of market-like behaviours into the system (or systems, as until devolution in 1998, Scottish, Welsh and Northern Irish HE formed constituent parts of the UK system). This analysis does not dwell on the influence of individual universities, powerful lobbying agents as they can be alongside their representative 'mission groups' in the policy-making process, although their influence can often be divined in finalised policy; nor does this book have anything to say on research policy or internationalisation. The emphasis here is on pro-market arguments employed by governments to impact institutional behaviour in relation to undergraduate provision in the context of a relatively autonomous sector by global comparison (Huisman, Meek, & Wood, 2007).

Nevertheless, successive governments have usually been able to cajole a national body of (often but not always reluctant) institutions to accept the gradual marketisation of their sector through a combination of a single regulatory and funding framework and a series of fiscal incentives reflecting changing policy priorities. The purpose of this analysis, however, is not to present a narrative historical account of 'one damn funding incentive after another'; rather it aims to explore arguments behind policy that account for the ways in which marketisation has been used to create the highly complex differentiated system we have today. Given the focus on arguments and rationalisation of policy, the analytical approach is PDA. The book identifies five main stages of marketisation policy (Table I.1), which attempt to frame the development of and continuing application of many of the arguments in the policy discourse briefly outlined here:

Any in-depth analysis of English marketisation policy cannot be complete without contextual explanatory factors. Policy statements and legislative changes appear sometimes contradictory and certainly do not represent a linear trajectory from a simple state-mandated command system to a free-for-all. Each of the policy stages identified above can be seen as influenced by key external drivers. These include:

- the establishment of institutional mission groups (from 1994);
- neoliberal ideology (a global predilection for market solutions);
- domestic institutional league tables (from 2005);
- 2008 crash and the consequent ramifications for public spending; and
- 2015 onwards – growing perception that 'there may be too many people going to university'.

The presence of these external factors in the policy domain shows the extent to which policy statements are often reactive, and questions the notion that the 'neoliberal marketisation' of such systems is designedly linear. The analysis is presented in three chapters covering the five stages outlined above and in a concluding chapter which presents the overall

Table I.1. The Cumulative Effect of Marketisation Discourse.

Stage 1: 1986–1992	Stage 2: 1992–2000	Stage 3: 2000–2010	Stage 4: 2010–2015	Stage 5: 2015–
Efficiency and accountability; human capital	Efficiency and accountability; human capital; diversity as a good	Diversity as a good; efficiency and accountability; human capital; differentiation	Diversity as a good; efficiency and accountability; human capital; differentiation; competition on price and quality	Diversity as a good; efficiency and accountability; human capital; differentiation; competition on price and quality; risk and exit

analysis and discusses the findings in the context of what they can tell us about the nature of neoliberalism.

CHAPTERISATION

Chapter 1 'The Genesis of Market Reforms: Efficiency, Accountability and the Celebration of Diversity' traces policy development from the earliest uses of market-like concepts in HE in the 1980s and incorporates the Further and Higher Education (F&HE) Act 1992 (HMSO, 1992) which 'freed up' (incorporated) further education colleges (FECs) and state-run HE colleges and polytechnics. It covers the first two 'stages' of market reform: the 'efficiency and accountability' stage and the 'celebration of diversity' stage, both predicated on system growth and notions of human capital to meet the needs of the developing 'knowledge economy'. Key policy drivers here included the radically marketised discourses and policies of the third-term Conservative government (elected in 1987) expressed in New Public Management theories and the international competitive realisation that human capital would be increasingly important in a post-industrial labour market (Hood, 1995). Participation in higher and further education therefore had to be increased (and necessarily widened), but increasingly the costs of the system also had to be made accountable and more efficient. The chapter proceeds to explore how system diversity slowly morphed into differentiation with the introduction of tensions within the enlarged sector around notions of quality and purpose expressed in the formation of mission groups representing the older universities. The Russell Group and the 1994 Group mission groups were both established in 1994, with the express purpose of differentiating themselves from what became known as post-1992 or 'new' universities. These tensions were also expressed in the public debates around the Dearing Review (NCIHE, 1997) which rationalised the introduction of tuition fees (legislated for by the incoming Labour government in 1997) and state funding of efforts to widen participation. Fees and widening participation (WP) policy were to become the locus of further differentiation in two ways: first, it was older institutions that were keenest to lobby for variable tuition fees (on the assumption that only they would justify a higher fee because what they provided was of greater value); second, as state-funded WP developed, it became clear that pre- and post-1992 universities had quite different aims and priorities based on their different needs in relation to the selection or recruitment of students.

Chapter 2 'From Diversity to Differentiation: The Coming of the Market' covers the third and fourth major stages of marketisation, spanning the period from 2000 to 2015, as differentiation is encouraged in order for HE institutions (HEIs) to be more competitive in the arenas of quality and price. The third stage encompasses the 2003 White Paper and Higher Education Act 2004, which introduced variable fees and the market in financial support bursaries, both overtly designed to enable differentiation. The fourth stage – the introduction of price and quality to the differentiation already in place – incorporated the trebling of variable fees in 2010, thus transferring the entire cost of HE to the graduate as recommended by the Browne Review of Student Finance (2010) and the White Paper *Students at the Heart of the System* (DBIS, 2011). This White Paper both rationalised and justified the raising of the tuition fee cap to £9,000 per year of study and attempted to deal with the ramifications for public spending created by the setting of fees by institutions at a far higher rate than predicted (government modelling had suggested the system would be cost-neutral). Central to both tasks was the increasing focus on choice based on information and a series of incentives to change applicant behaviour. This approach was based on the assumption that many well-qualified young people from disadvantaged backgrounds were failing to maximise their opportunities by applying to institutions that demanded the highest University and College Application System (UCAS) tariff points for entry (a notion first identified as a social mobility deficit by the Sutton Trust report *The Missing 3000* in 2004).

In order to introduce differentiation based on quality and price, the 2011 White Paper established a complex set of student number control (SNC) incentives designed to encourage institutions to increase the number of high UCAS tariff applicants within their capped number of students at the expense of those less qualified. The declared intention (Taylor & McCaig, 2014) was to concentrate the best qualifying students in a smaller number of institutions (HEFCE, 2011), as better-informed applicants responded to the opportunity to study at higher-status institutions. The flip-side of this would be that lower-status institutions would lose better-qualified students and respond by competing among themselves, on price, for additional student numbers. Indeed, additional places were created for any HE provider willing to offer undergraduate places at £7,500 or below, a move designed to increase competitive pressure by expanding the number of HE providers from among FECs and new alternative providers (Evans, 2015, 2016; HEA, 2014; McCaig & Taylor, 2016). This extraordinary set of market levers represented a short-lived experiment (abandoned after two academic years) that conceptually took systemic differentiation to a new level, but also revealed the paucity of options to tackle the twin problems of having put the cost decisions in the hands of (unreliable) applicant-consumers, and the understandable tendency of HEIs to charge as much as they could for as long as they could, before any market effect forced them to set lower fees. In recognition of the failure of the 'high grades' SNC regime, government decided to abolish number controls completely (in a surprise Budget announcement, HM Treasury, 2013) and put their faith in a demand-led open market (from 2015 to 2016) and promised legislation to encourage new providers to market: thereafter it was assumed that the supply of undergraduate places would finally meet (and perhaps exceed) demand.

Chapter 3 'The Higher Education and Research Act 2017: The Road to Risk and Exit' represents a fifth stage of marketisation – the application of risk and exit, managed by a newly enhanced market regulator. This chapter contextualises the regulatory changes necessary to finally realise the opening up of the HE market. This was largely designed to encourage new 'challenger' providers who would henceforth be part of the same regulatory 'level playing field' for the first time (Bowl, McCaig, & Hughes, 2018). The new phase of marketisation went further than mere regulatory reforms: for the first time the risk of institutional failure was contemplated; no longer would financially embarrassed institutions be encouraged to merge and in effect be propped up by government via funding council student number allocations. Like any other competitive body in a capitalist system, they would be allowed to go into administration, and as part of the costs of a risk-based system they would also have to offer to compensate students still enrolled and have entered into credit-transfer agreements with other local providers so that those students could complete their studies.

Alongside these measures to increase the competitive differentiation of the English system, the introduction of a Teaching Excellence Framework (TEF) (the subject of a separate volume in this series, French and O'Leary, 2017) seems designed to impact the market in a more subtle way. Born of the long-held belief that teaching and learning are seen as less important than research within the HE system, the introduction of Gold, Silver and Bronze TEF ratings of teaching excellence acts as another piece of information for applicant-consumers who were previously confronted with league tables and other esteem markers based largely on research income and UCAS tariff requirements as proxies for quality. Initial TEF ratings showed (to no one's surprise) that excellent teaching is not distributed among HE providers in the same pattern as research excellence (DfE, 2017), and to that extent the TEF had the opportunity to be a subversive and even disruptive addition to the debate about what makes 'a good university'. However, plans to introduce variable fee caps based on TEF ratings were subsequently dropped (WonkHE, 2018) perhaps in recognition that the greater possibilities of price differential as a result of market competition would render the TEF link contradictory and confusing, given that TEF ratings are benchmarked by institution type.

Chapter 4 'Continuity and Discontinuity on the Road to Risk and Exit: Stages of Marketisation in Comparative Policy Analysis' presents a thematic overview of the varied and contingent trajectories of English marketisation policy over the 30-year period. Revisiting the five stages in their wider context allows for a deeper analysis of their development: rather than arguments for marketisation replacing each other, what this analysis reveals is the ways that arguments are retained and built upon as the basis for subsequent arguments, sometimes reappearing in different forms. For example, the first-stage arguments about 'efficiency and accountability' in the name of human capital maximisation, while always in the background during the 'competitive differentiation' period, reappeared during the final stage as government sought to shift the responsibility for public expenditure onto institutions and applicants (exhorting applicants to think carefully whether it is worth taking on debt in excess of the financial returns from low-remunerative degree programmes) (DfE, 2016). Similarly, 'diversity', which was initially evoked as a celebration of the newly unified system after 1992 but then subsumed within 'differentiation', is reimagined in the most recent reform stage as a justification for innovative new providers to enter the market. Differentiation, once encouraged in discourse and by the introduction of variable fees in the early 2000s, plays an even more central role on the register of reputational 'risk', based as the system is on heightened regulation. HE providers will henceforth be differentiated not only by their teaching excellence (TEF) but also by their likelihood of having to undergo quality assurance checks, with the 'better performing' (and thus less at risk) providers left largely to their own devices.

This concluding chapter will also re-examine what this marketisation trajectory can tell us about the nature of neoliberalisation by examining some of the external factors that have shaped this particular system. This analysis reveals a number of policy drivers external to any intended marketisation project. Some of these policy drivers appear as unintended consequences that were not prefigured in legislation: rapid differentiation within the sector (following the unification of the sector in 1992); the introduction of tuition fees in 1998 (responding to an economic need to replace previous cuts); the publication of institutional league tables (initially by the *Times Higher Education* in 2005); the heightened need to control public spending after the crash of 2008 (which led to the shifting of the whole cost of tuition onto students); and the subsequent need to shape applicant behaviour to create a price differential that would reduce average fees to the affordable level (of £7,500 per year). This continued to the extent that by 2017 government was encouraging new providers to the market at the same time as questioning the return on investment for some young people if they elected to sign up to some of the new provision government had encouraged into being. At each stage of development of what some might see as a steady and inevitable neoliberal marketisation process, in this analysis management of the system is revealed to be more of a contingent juggling act, with governments reacting to unplanned circumstances with often short-term 'solutions'. So, what in the end does this say about the neoliberal system? In order to explore these key issues, the book uses a specific framing of neoliberalism and market differentiation and employs a PDA approach.

NEOLIBERAL DIFFERENTIATION

Marketisation as Part of the Neoliberal Imaginary

English HE has become steadily more subject to market competition and in many ways has become the most market-oriented HE system in global comparison, accompanied by the highest average tuition fees outside of the HE market in the United States. The marketisation of HE systems is a global phenomenon that has attracted a high level of scholarly research employing theoretical concepts ranging from academic capitalism to neoliberalism. To what extent, then, is the English system 'neoliberal' and if the system can be so characterised, what can it tell us about the nature and perhaps the future direction of the neoliberalisation of systems in general? Much of the debate is focused on causation and trajectory. Differentiation is visible in two main aspects of HE policymaking in a system which has become increasingly marketised and diversified in the years since the 1992 Further and Higher Education Act (HMSO, 1992); the aspect relating to the needs and interests of HE providers and that relating to consumers of HE.

Differentiation is important for any HE provider wishing to position its 'offer' in relation to other providers; this can be manifest either in individualised or in collective terms. For example, older 'pre-1992' universities not only aim to differentiate themselves from each other for competitive reasons (given that they may broadly select applicants from the same national and international pool), but as a grouping they seek differentiation in relation to newer post-1992 universities and other providers. Differentiation of this kind is important within a national regulatory system such as has emerged in the UK and (particularly since devolution in 1998) in England. International comparisons (e.g. Huisman et al., 2007) found that the English HE system was the most diverse of the countries studied. They noted that 'although the formal binary divide disappeared, many differences have continued to exist between the "old" and "new" universities, and that these differences were maintained through government-driven market mechanisms' which encouraged mission-diversity rather than state planning (Huisman et al., 2007, p. 574).

Differentiation between and among providers can manifest horizontally, for example by subject discipline (specialised or broad), by mode of delivery (work-based learning, part-time), by mission (as 'access' institutions or those aiming to maintain the 'world class reputation' of English HE). Equally, and especially since the introduction of variable tuition fees (2004 HE Act) and the publication of institutional league tables and other consumerist guides (*Which? University;* the *Good University Guide*) based on selected metrics of performance (including the entry qualifications required), differentiation can be represented vertically with all regulated providers expressed as a list with those deigned 'better' at the top of the distribution.

This shift away from an appreciation of a broad and diverse set of HE institutions that satisfied different wants of different student groups and employers to a simple linear hierarchy is seen as a threat to the project of WP to groups historically under-represented (e.g. Archer, 2007), and the relative immobility of this hierarchy severely curtails the opportunity for social mobility for students at lower-ranked institutions (Boliver, 2011). Such linearity of the system drives differentiation as expressed in statements of institutional positionality and mission (Bowl & Hughes, 2013; Graham, 2013; McCaig, 2015, 2016) that confirm differentiated approaches to widening access to HE, in turn reflective of their respective student intakes. Government incentives to further drive differentiation in respect of tuition fee variance and by concentrating the highest-qualified applicants in the highest-ranked institutions, such as the High Grades SNC policy (DBIS, 2011, discussed in Chapter 3) also reinforce and oblige (re)positionality in the form of tariff points demanded by the UCAS. Indeed, one of the few ways that institutions can move up the league tables is by increasing the UCAS points required. Once again, given the well-documented links between social class deprivation and educational attainment (Archer, 2003a, 2003b; DBIS, 2015; HEFCE, 2010; OFFA, 2010; Social Mobility Commission, 2016; The Sutton Trust, 2004), differentiation from HE providers' perspective enables the highest-ranked institutions to more easily select applicants most likely to seamlessly maintain the provider's prestige and world ranking. Other, less successful providers are thus left with the less prestigious role of 'WP'.

From the applicant-as-consumer point of view, differentiation is important to the decision-making process. A consistent argument throughout the various policy statements analysed in this book is that since the introduction of variable fees and especially since the financial crash of 2008, the onus is on the individual to optimise her/his choice of HE course, and the mechanism for this is information (DBIS, 2011;

Sellar, 2013). In the English (indeed UK-wide) system of applications for school-leavers, UCAS enables any applicant to apply to study on any course at any institution they believe they will be qualified for, based on predicted grades. There is a UCAS tariff which enables a comparison of equivalent qualifications and required grades and which functions, in the absence of actual variation in tuition fees, as the effective price differential that drives supply and demand in the system. Demand for places from suitably qualified applicants at the highest-tariff institutions exceeds supply, enabling such providers to be selective; at lower tariff points, on any given degree programme, the supply of places is less restricted and lower-ranked institutions are usually obliged to compete among similar institutions to recruit students. The consumer in this market then chooses a degree programme they can 'afford' to 'purchase' when their actual grades are attained in the same way any retail consumer chooses the version of a product or service that she/he can afford at the time.

While tuition fee variation is still largely absent from the market (fees in 2017–2018 were clustered very close to the £9,250 maximum), applicants are expected to make use of a variety of data that help make explicit what is widely held to be implicit — that some HE providers and degree programmes are more desirable from the point of view of future financial and career success for the individual. Conversely, of course, there are some providers and programmes that are less remunerative. Key Information Sets which combine data on student satisfaction (the National Student Survey), the expected employability of graduates from a given course (Destination of Leavers from HE survey) and other aspects of the programme such as guided teaching hours, are to be augmented by subject-level TEF ratings and a calculation of Longitudinal Educational Outcomes (LEO). It is those applicants who fail to aim for the highest possible course who are most likely to progress into employment that does not lead to the full repayment of their loans. That becomes a problem for government spending of course, which is why government strives to create a system whereby differential outcomes are reflected in differential tuition fees to create a dual-price mechanism. This, it is assumed, will lead to applicants eschewing less remunerative courses, forcing providers to lower their costs to maintain 'market share'. While the individual applicant-consumer has a large role in this process (albeit hampered by a reluctance among many to aim as 'high' as they could), a further level of differentiation has most recently been encouraged on the supply side – the removal of the cap on student places (HM Treasury, 2013) and the active encouragement of many more new providers to the market (HM Government, 2017). How could such a differentiated system fit within the rubric of neoliberalism?

A Definition of Neoliberalism in the English HE Context

While it is now commonplace to link the market reforms discussed in this volume, and the Labour, Coalition and Conservative governments that introduced them, in a seamless narrative of neoliberalism, this book questions those assumptions. Neoliberalism, most commonly defined as the encouragement of market mechanisms in public HE (e.g. Agasisti & Catalano, 2006; Brown & Carrasso, 2014; Lynch, 2006; Marginson, 2013; McGettigan, 2013; Meek, 2000; Ka Ho Mok, 1999; Molesworth, Nixon, & Scullion, 2010; Paulsen & St John, 2002; Sellar, 2013; Varman, Saha, & Skålén, 2011), is often employed as a high-level concept not necessarily designed for, or amenable to, empirical analysis. Undefined, neoliberalism can become little more than a catch-all trope rather than a hypothesis to be tested.

As a result, many causal factors behind policy change must be considered. These include the drive for international competitiveness in the face of globalisation, public financial crises and the business interests of institutions – which are external to the specific and deliberate control of governments designing a supposedly coherent neoliberal system.

This study is based on a specific definition of neoliberalism in the context of English HE; the theoretical 'neoliberal market model for higher education' (Marginson, 2013) is based on the assumption that the market is the most effective and efficient distributor of goods and services (Agasisti & Catalano, 2006; Brown & Carasso, 2014; Lynch, 2006; Newman & Jahdi, 2009). However, it is well understood that markets in HE are very different from perfect competition models (Agasisti & Catalano, 2006; Brown & Carasso, 2014; Marginson, 2013; McGettigan, 2013; Molesworth et al., 2010) and that neoliberalism in this context instead implies the use of market incentives by governments within a regulated system in an effort to change behaviours, be they institutional, academic or student behaviours (McCaig & Taylor, 2017).

A neoliberal HE system – exemplified by the English case – implies a demand-led application process within a regulated system established by the state to match demand for places (what applicants want to study and the level of tuition fees they are willing to pay) with supply (the number of places and nature of provision offered by providers). However, this has never been as linear a process as some might envisage. Considering the 'efficiency and accountability' stage of reforms in 1988 (the subject of Chapter 1), Walford found that:

> *Recent British government policy on higher*
> *education has not been totally coherent. For*
> *example, there have been measures instituting*

> *increased central control that contradict the main thrust towards privatisation which has been identified in this article. However, the ideology of privatisation has been a decisive influence in the way government policy on higher education has evolved in the last eight or nine years, and it may also be argued that the process of privatisation demands increased government control in the short term to establish the new system (Walford, 1988, p. 60).*

While Walford clearly identified the encouragement of market-like incentives imported from the business world and the gathering of powers by the state, which we would today recognise as neoliberalism, it was in his analysis designed to be a temporary phenomenon. Perhaps it was; retrospection can often confound post hoc theoretical analyses that search for logical coherence in public policymaking. So what can we say about the system that has evolved in these 30 years?

The English neoliberal tuition fee system, it seems, takes a middle ground between a freely privatised market and the continuation of state planning. Rather, it is designed with several key characteristics in place: to encourage the individualised responsibilisation of risk in the labour market; to reduce public exposure to debt (because the state underwrites tuition fees and thus carries the risk of non-repayment), yet at the same time to ensure the system is responsive to labour market needs and the national economic imperative. It consists of some market incentives but is contained within a regulatory system to control the overall quality, size and shape of the sector. A neoliberal HE system is thus an alternative to a truly open market driven by an 'invisible hand' (Meek, 2000) which no government controls and no system contains; in this definition, the United States, which has over 4000 HE providers, none of which are subject to the same degree or level of regulation by any national structure, is an example of an open market rather than a neoliberal system. Neoliberalism, from the outside, is a contained market – contained by a system of policy levers operated by the state. Internally, neoliberalism is manifested as the application of selected market incentives in order to shape preferences and outcomes, bounded by a single regulatory framework.

Neoliberalism, thus defined, can make use of various policy imperatives: human capitalism, WP, social mobility, social justice or any other variant of policy required by the state to meet its ends. It could justify the celebration of an elite and the reintroduction of a binary divide. It could pick winners and concentrate research funding, even without the apparatus of apparent competition such as Research Excellence Framework (REF) or the TEF (Sellar, 2013). The key questions, from the point of policy analysis, are why do states select some policies and not others; and what constrains them from other options?

It is the recognition of constraining factors that reveals the continuing importance of non-state actors; where do they fit in the supposedly monolithic neoliberal apparatus? What drives institutions? What drives the publishers of league tables? What role is there for the influence of economic and marketing theory? What role for the internationalisation of HE in response to the globalisation of economies? Does monolithic neoliberalism have anything to say about all these elements? This book traces policy development over three decades culminating in the Higher Education and Research Act (HMSO, 2017), yet this latter Act attempts to introduce much more freedom into the market in a way that potentially challenges our working definition of a neoliberal HE system. If neoliberalism in HE is typified by a focus only on narrow measurable market outcomes (Lynch, 2006) or purely in the name of economic efficiency (Agasisti & Catalano, 2006), the new regulatory requirements for accreditation in England ensure that maximisation of economic value is not in fact the only goal.

Rewarding teaching excellence, for example in the form of TEF ratings, potentially threatens the existing market hierarchy of institutions (as exemplified by league tables) by changing the definition of what constitutes excellence. Can this be said to challenge the notion of a neoliberal system in which the state holds all the regulatory cards, or does it merely represent a shuffling of levers? Similarly, post-legislative changes to the operation of the HERA regime exempted new challenger providers from many of its prohibitively expensive strictures; does this mean that competition from outwith the regulatory system is designed to act on institutions within the system? That might make the regime more of a market than a neoliberal system as here defined. The most recent reforms are also reliant on a much lighter-touch, risk-based regulatory system (to the extent that will not protect providers from exiting the market) which may question the ability of the system to contain the market within the state's boundaries. Other definitions of neoliberalism stress its 'amorphous' nature consisting a 'complex, often incoherent, unstable and even contradictory set of practices' (Shamir, 2008, p. 3) with the potential of blurring the boundaries between economy and society. We will re-examine the relationship between neoliberalism and the English variant in the concluding discussion.

Approaches to Policy Discourse Analysis

This book employs a PDA approach to examine the development of marketisation policy over time and in the guise of a dozen policy statements over the 30-year period since 1986.

PDA (Fairclough & Fairclough, 2013) differs from the more established critical discourse analysis (CDA) approach. CDA is a useful tool for comparative analysis of statutory policy statements that follow an established format, such as Office for Fair Access (OFFA) agreements or TEF submissions, because their purpose is to establish positionality in relation to a specific set of issues the regulatory body has identified (Bowl & Hughes, 2013; Graham, 2013; McCaig, 2015). Equally it can be used to compare non-statutory but formal sites of communication and positionality, as employed by Fairclough (1993) when comparing the discourses used in academic recruitment advertisements placed by old and new universities.

Criticality can be employed in the analysis of these documents if the research purpose is to identity variation by issues such as responsibility or ownership (often visible in the changing use of pronouns) and particularly if such responsibilisation is shifting over time (e.g. in multiple documents from the same institution) or between institution types, for example a tendency for one specific type of HE provider to establish positionality in relation to quality or access that can be used to differentiate it from other providers or types of provider. CDA is useful as it employs the market notion of positionality as a projection that takes institutions and organisations beyond their essence (Foucault 1972, 1979); a projection enables positionality in the marketplace of ideas and values (Fairclough, 1993; Gibbs & Knapp, 2002). It accepts that there are varied types of 'goods' (definitions of utility of an HE institution) and that the application of positioning and repositioning in the marketplace for these goods can be contained in the discourses employed.

While CDA is a useful tool for analysis of institutional responses to policy incentives, the ambition of this book is to analyse the policies themselves and the arguments employed to justify policy change. It thus uses political discourse analysis (Fairclough & Fairclough, 2013) which is an approach that recognises that governments have a far greater degree of freedom than institutions' repositioning along a set of predetermined market tracks. Critical PDA is also more appropriate in this instance because the documents subject to analysis do not share the characteristics of fixed responsive position statements over time and in direct comparison to documents submitted by all providers to the same regulatory body, as is the case with OFFA agreements or TEF submissions, nor are they periodically reissued to enable comparison (and positional change) over time.

The policy documents critically analysed in the following three chapters of this book are variously government-sponsored reviews and reports, Green Papers, White Papers and Acts of Parliament. They appear at different times in the last three decades of UK and English HE policy, in response to different issues, and they have different audiences and purposes. They are not documents establishing (or shifting) market positionality within a fixed frame of reference; they are arguments to justify the reformation of policy, to change the frame of reference. Government has to persuade; in essence these policy statements reflect problems identified, either politically (in response to internal party pressures) or in wider terms of responding to new requirements of the system (e.g. in response to global trends, real or ideological). PDA thus allows the researcher to analyse the gestation and trajectory of system-level policy, and in turn reveal the extent of the influences of competing ideologies, longer-term economic policy imperatives, and also the constraining factors represented by other non-governmental actors. In the case of the policy documents that are the subject of this book, critical PDA helps us reveal the varying — and non-linear — ways that successive governments have introduced and rationalised marketisation policies into the English system. Set in their appropriate context, this series of policy reforms reveal the shifting understanding of what the marketisation of the English HE system could mean, which set of levers would most appropriately enable the desired outcomes (at any given moment) and, most importantly, they reveal the role of other factors and, by extension, the paucity of monolithic neoliberalism as an analytical tool. Neoliberalism is shown to be merely a framing device for often reactive policymaking; in itself, I will argue, neoliberalism as a meta-discourse contributes relatively little to our understanding of the success or failure of marketisation arguments.

This book will now proceed to look at the first two of the five stages of marketisation (Chapter 1), followed by stages three and four (Chapter 2) and fuller analysis of the fifth and final stage (Chapter 3) before concluding with an overall analytical discussion chapter.

CHAPTER 1

THE GENESIS OF MARKET REFORMS: EFFICIENCY, ACCOUNTABILITY AND THE CELEBRATION OF DIVERSITY

1.1. INTRODUCTION

While the main focus of this book is the three major White Papers and two Acts of Parliament of the early twenty-first century, the intellectual roots of marketisation can be traced back to the Conservative governments of the 1980s and 1990s. This chapter covers the first two stages of marketisation – the 'accountability and efficiency stage' which emerged in the late 1980s, and the 'diversity as good' stage, covering the period 1992 to 2000.

During the 1980s, the HE system was expected to begin expanding again after a period of retrenchment and stagnation after the inflationary crises of the 1970s. The OPEC crisis had led to the quadrupling of oil prices and subsequent public spending cuts, leading to a fall in the numbers of people attending HE for the first time since the Second World

War (DES, 1978; Kogan & Kogan, 1983, p. 25). Overall, university funding had failed to keep pace with inflation during the 1974–1981 period, with a cut-off of 10% in per-student funding (Walford, 1988, p. 48). Growth was reignited during the mid-1980s, partly stimulated by even more radical cuts (17% across the sector announced in the 1981 Budget) with the University Governing Council steering the process, favouring institutions that would expand the numbers studying subjects of importance to the economy — science, technology and engineering — while cutting places for social sciences and the humanities. In order to survive this level of funding cuts, Polytechnics and colleges took the opportunity to absorb unmet demand by accepting larger numbers of students at a lower 'unit-of-resource' per student, thus rapidly becoming the locus of most of the late-1980s expansion. By 1985, Polytechnics were for the first time teaching more than half of all full-time UK students (Robertson, 1995; Walford, 1988).

The government were also reacting to international competition and a demographic shortfall (expected to last until 1995) in the number of young applicants (18-year-olds for standard entry) by expanding places for mature students (DES, 1986). Most of the ensuing growth in student numbers occurred in the Polytechnics and larger Colleges of HE — the public sector of HE — rather than the universities. This inevitably implied a widening of participation to social groups that had little previous experience of accessing HE. Following a period of rapid growth from the late 1980s (young people's participation more than doubled under Kenneth Baker 1988–1992), the 1992 Further and Higher Education Act abolished the binary divide between universities and Polytechnics, creating a unified and diverse sector of around 130 institutions that remains largely unchanged today, albeit added to by new 'challenger providers' (DBIS, 2016a, 2016b).

This chapter explores both these developments as aspects of the development of marketisation.

1.2. ACCOUNTABILITY AND EFFICIENCY

During the early and mid-1980s, secure Conservative governments — influenced by new right ideological thought — were encouraging the use of market principles for the allocation of public resources in the name of greater accountability and efficiency in state-funded services. This was an example of New Public Management Theory in practice (the use of private sector practices in the public sector of the economy, Hood, 1995) and national economic competitiveness, employing 'human capital' economic theories to counter emerging globalisation. Human capital conceptually describes the econometric link between education and employment; in the UK context, its usage is rooted in the changing basis of industrial demand for labour, the comparative decline of the UK economy and the growing inequality of income since the late 1960s (Barnett, 1986; Evans, 1992; Glennerster & Hills, 1998; Wiener, 1981). It should be reiterated, of course, that the state's interest in making the HE system more accountable and efficient, not least in providing for an improvement in the maximisation of the nation's human capital, was reflected in the Robbins Report, and indeed would become ever more important in the context of the systemic growth he recommended (Robbins, 1963). These manifestations implied a need for governments to centralise powers over the education system, firstly in order to reduce the amount of inter-party political dispute about the means and ends of the system, given that the public sector of HE (the Polytechnics and Colleges of HE) was controlled by local authorities, often Labour-led, and secondly to maximise economic outcomes in the face of international competition.

The starting point for analysis of the Conservative reforms of the 1980s, therefore, is a recognition of greater state involvement in the HE system throughout the post-WWII era. While during the pre-war period the proportion of income universities received from the state via the University Grants Committee (UGC) never exceeded 30% of their overall income, this situation changed rapidly after 1945:

> *After the war, the need for a rapid expansion caused this to rise to about 50% in 1946, to over 70% from 1953, and to about 90% for most of the universities in 1980. Such major changes in the degree to which universities were dependent on government funding meant that there were inevitably corresponding changes in the UGC's role (Walford, 1988, 48).*

These changes at ideological level were to be manifested in two key reports that in turn impacted on the development of legislation leading to the ending of the binary divide in 1992.

1.3. JARRATT AND CROHAM: THE BUSINESS CASE FOR ACCOUNTABILITY AND EFFICIENCY

In April 1984, the Committee of Vice-Chancellors and Principals (CVCP) appointed the Jarratt Committee to investigate university efficiency. This was designed as an attempt to convince the UGC and the government that the universities were taking the demands for greater efficiency seriously, given the context that the UGC had signalled less funding for universities after 1984. The 12 members of the Jarratt Committee included four industrialists and the Prime

Minister's efficiency adviser, alongside six representatives of the universities (Walford, 1988, p. 55). Among the key findings of the final report (Jarratt, 1985) were that universities were to be run by Chief Executive Officers (or Vice-Chancellors acting in that manner) and that performance indicators were to be introduced alongside staff development, appraisal and accountability.

Further, Jarratt recommended that the Department for Education and Skills conduct a review of the UGC's role, staffing and structure. This reported as the Croham Report (1987), recommending that the UGC 'construct a national strategy for the investment of public funds' in universities, and to exercise close and effective oversight over the 'financial competence' of individual universities (Croham, 1987). It was led by 'an eminent figure with substantial experience outside the academic world combined with a strong personal interest in higher education', and a full-time executive director general, who 'should have had substantial experience of high office in a university' (Walford, 1988, p. 56). This helped preserve the notion that the reformed UGC would be seen as both independent and effective:

> *It was to be more active and managerial, but the grants, once given, were still to be block grants to individual universities. Croham supported the need for flexibility at the local level, and wished to avoid 'excessive concentration of decision-making with the UGC'. Block grants, rather than a series of item-specific grants, were seen as important to retain academic freedom, to avoid too much government influence on the detailed workings of the universities, and as being the most likely way of obtaining the greatest internal efficiency (Walford, 1988, p. 57).*

The revised UGC should have overall control of conditions of grants to universities and require greater accountability from the latter as to the disposal of their fiscal allocations. Croham also recommended the introduction of a triennial funding system, ensuring adequate time for institutions to plan necessary changes in the event of fiscal reduction (Walford, 1988, p. 91).

Much of the Croham Report was reflected in the White Paper *Higher Education: Meeting the Challenge* (DES, 1987), published prior to the 1987 General Election (when the Conservative government was returned for a third term). However, as Walford points out, there were some significant changes that went beyond Croham, showing that the government wished to replace the UGC with a University Funding Council (UFC) whose 'essential responsibilities should relate to the allocation of funding between universities rather than to its overall amount, which is a matter for Government to decide after considering all the evidence' (Walford, 1988, p. 56). In future, the payment of UFC grants to institutions would take the form of a contractual relationship between institutions (as service providers) and the UFC as the consumer. Instead of a UGC with advisory powers, the UFC was to be purely a funding allocator acting on behalf of (but at arms' length from) government. Instead of being suppliers of HE funded by block grants, universities would become competing suppliers of those services demanded by the consumer.

According to drafts of the 1987 Bill (Walford, 1988), contracts would be introduced which would enhance both accountability (to the public purse) and entrepreneurial dimensions designed to:

(a) encourage institutions to be enterprising in attracting contracts from other sources, particularly the private

sector, and thereby to lessen their existing degree of
dependence on public funding;

(b) sharpen accountability for the use of the public funds which would continue to be required;

(c) strengthen the commitment of institutions to the delivery of the educational services which they agree with the new planning and funding bodies to provide.

Sir Peter Swinnerton-Dyer, Chairman of the UGC, made the extent of the change clear:

> *Ministers are no longer thinking in terms of grants, however calculated, but in terms of buying certain services from universities. The bulk of those services are research and teaching. The Government is here a single purchaser, faced with an array of competing suppliers. It will use the power which that situation gives to press for greater efficiency, just as Marks and Spencer, for example, does in similar circumstances, indeed, it is already starting to do so. (Reported in* The Times Educational Supplement, *2 October 1987, p. 17., in Walford, 1988, p. 59.)*

Henceforth, HE's links with the corporate world would be strengthened, and its contribution to economic growth more fully asserted. Human capital thinking clearly played a dominant role as the White Paper linked growth (and by necessity wider access to HE) to the need for highly qualified manpower. In the service of a better balance between the needs of the economy and the needs of individuals, improvements in the management, performance and accountability of the individual institutions would drive quality and efficiency (DES, 1987). The White Paper also suggested the removal of the 'public sector' of HE from local authority control. Such large institutions of HE were to be placed under a Polytechnic and Colleges Funding Council (PCFC) as an equivalent body to the UFC.

The extended role of the state also affected the universities. Academic tenure was formally abolished to ensure that institutions would have the power to terminate the appointment of academic staff for reasons of redundancy or financial exigency (both terms for the first time defined in legislation). Critically, reference was made to dismissal for 'good cause', which refers to unsatisfactory performance of duties (Dennison, 1989, p. 93). This would open the way for newly empowered university managers to change the nature of their provision against the wishes of academics. While opposition to the Bill in the House of Lords (led by the CVCP) ensured that 'academic freedom' was enshrined in legislation, as Dennison noted: 'the government's action is consistent with its vision of universities as institutions able to respond to economic needs and to changes in the corporate marketplace' (Dennison, 1989, p. 93). In a prescient conclusion, Dennison foresaw the link between market forces and state-mandated neoliberalism:

> *While there is more direct government influence over the operations of the college sectors, universities are by no means immune. Contemporary political jurisdictions have a tendency to intrude into the operation of any or all social institutions under the rhetoric of economic reform and the pursuit of market-driven priorities (Dennison, 1989, p. 96).*

The subsequent 1988 Education Reform Act legislated for the 29 Polytechnics and with them all colleges with 350 or more full-time equivalent HE students and more than 55% of full-time equivalent students in HE courses (around

30 colleges) to be incorporated as PCFC institutions. Dennison (1989) summarised the new regime:

> *The individual polytechnics and colleges, under their new corporate status, will operate with both a governing and an academic board. A high degree of accountability will be expected from the governing boards, which will be broadly representative of both internal and external groups. The Secretary of State will retain certain powers regarding the initial selection of outside representatives. The role and responsibility of community groups in influencing postsecondary educational policy has clearly been reduced. It might be argued that good educational management is the ultimate objective but few deny that one overt political motive is the government's wish to undermine the power of unsympathetic local politicians (Dennison, 1989, p. 95).*

This contemporary summary encapsulates both the ideological and political motivations in play. Increased accountability and links to the national economic imperative (the enhanced role for employers on boards) is evidence of human capital economic theory in application and more widely of what we came to think of as neoliberalism. However, the needs of the Conservative central state to override local and community resistance to its marketisation rhetoric implied an overtly political agenda to assert market hegemony by the removal of alternative voices and power bases. Walford's equally prescient conclusion noted the incoherence of policy; the state had mandated 'a thrust towards privatisation', reflecting that:

> *[T]he ideology of privatisation has been a decisive influence in the way government policy on higher*

education has evolved in the last eight or nine years, and it may also be argued that the process of privatisation demands increased government control in the short term to establish the new system (Walford, 1988, p. 60).

Hence these earlier moves towards the marketisation of the system can be seen as neoliberal, a strong state regulatory system operating market levers to steer the behaviour of participating actors within that system.

1.4. THE SECOND STAGE OF MARKETISATION: THE COMING AND CELEBRATION OF SYSTEM DIVERSITY

The establishment and subsequent abolition of a binary divide between institutions offering HE are key markers in the development of the English variant of marketisation. The binary divide, confirmed by Labour Secretary of State Anthony Crosland in a speech at Woolwich Polytechnic on the 27 April 1965, was specifically intended to control that part of HE output which government thought necessary to meet its economic and industrial needs, and was introduced against the express wishes of the Robbins Report (Robbins, 1963). Because it was also intended to maintain the autonomy of the traditional university sector, the binary divide was welcomed by many in the universities as a signal that they could continue 'unreformed'. Whereas Robbins' recommendation of an expanding unitary system could have provided the basis for a broad democratic advance, the establishment of the Polytechnics as a distinct sector would forever consign them to a 'second division' (Simon, 1991, p. 249).

Crosland made a spirited case for a dual system of HE, largely on the basis that the Polytechnics would inevitably feel inferior to the universities even if they were within the same structure, 'becoming a permanent poor relation'. He also made the social democratic case that a substantial part of HE 'should be under social control, and directly responsive to social needs' (Simon, 1991, p. 248). International competitiveness was a further motor of policy. In this sense, the Polytechnics were to have a regional role linked to industry's needs and the employment needs of the local population. Prefiguring future battles over system differentiation, Crosland concluded his Woolwich speech with a rhetorical flourish: 'Let us now move away from our snobbish, caste-ridden hierarchical obsession with university status' (Simon, 1991, p. 249).

Two decades later, the need for democratic control over key aspects of the HE system was becoming highly politicised. A public sector reflecting regional employment needs implied a role for the Local Education Authorities, anathema to Conservative thinking in the 1980s which wanted not only to reduce the powers of the Labour opposition but also to enable — hence incorporation — Polytechnics and Colleges of HE to offer provision that satisfied latent demand in the system. So, while Crosland had believed that the Polytechnics had by 1972 established themselves and were not 'trying to beat them [the universities] at their own game. Rather they are playing a different game with a different set of rules' (Reisman, 1997, p. 86), the pro-market policy environment of the late 1980s specifically invited them to play the same game, latterly even to reinvent themselves as universities.

1.5. THE ABOLITION OF THE BINARY DIVIDE — THE 1992 FURTHER AND HIGHER EDUCATION ACT

In May 1991, the White Paper *Higher Education — A New Framework* (Cm 1541) proposed changes that would more directly impact the supply side of the new market system, the most significant of which was to be the abolition of the binary divide and the creation of a unitary system of HE. In March 1992, the Further and Higher Education Act (HMSO, 1992) was passed by Parliament, with responsibility for the whole sector passing to the Funding Councils in each national jurisdiction; in England the UFC and PCFC were replaced by the Higher Education Funding Council for England (HEFCE).

HEFCE's founding mission was to 'promote the quality and quantity of learning and research in higher education institutions, cost-effectively and with regard to national needs' (HEFCE, 1994, para 4.2). National economic – human capital – imperatives were central to this mission as HEFCE aimed to 'encourage institutions to build on their strengths and expand their local, regional, national and international roles' by way of:

> *the maintenance and development of high-quality and cost-effective institutions, providing for the education of students, the advancement of knowledge and the pursuit of scholarship, and, thereby, playing their parts in meeting national needs (HEFCE, 1994, para 5.2).*

These national efficiency aims were augmented by emphasis on institutions' role in the development of their home communities:

> *promoting an expanding role for institutions in regional and local life as widely recognised resource and advice centres which are readily accessible to appropriate institutions, organisations and individuals. (HEFCE, 1994, para 5.3)*

Equally, HEFCE was concerned about diversity and widening participation (WP), with aims to:

> *encourage diversity in the provision of higher education, a widening of access and greater opportunities; ... the promotion of the provision of quality higher education which is distinctive in emphasising personal development in relation to the world of work and the community. (HEFCE, 1994, para 5.4)*

This included a reiteration of the Robbins principle: 'the widening of access to this provision for all individuals who wish to benefit from it and have the necessary qualities to do so'. Overtly, HEFCE would achieve these aims by reinforcing institutional autonomy in the forms of:

> *encouraging institutions to exercise their autonomy to the maximum degree consistent with full accountability for their use of funds derived from the Council as provided by the Further and Higher Education Act 1992;*
>
> *supporting increased participation by students of all types and especially by members of groups which are currently under-represented in higher education;*
>
> *seeking the provision of a growing range of choices within the higher education sector for students, for organisations and for others seeking its services, with individual institutions identifying their particular strengths and opportunities and developing them accordingly. (HEFCE, 1994, para 5.3)*

1.6. DEARING AND THE NEW LABOUR GOVERNMENT: DIVERSITY WITH A DIFFERENTIAL PURPOSE

In 1996, the Conservative government established the National Committee of Inquiry into Higher Education (NCIHE) under Sir Ron Dearing. After the election of the Labour government in July 1997, this committee reported as *Higher Education in the Learning Society* and is perhaps most noted for its rationale for the introduction of self-funded tuition (fees were introduced in 1998). However, the Committee's wide-ranging scope included the future size and shape of the sector and the importance of maintaining equivalent quality across all institutions, both essential factors in the development of a market, and views were solicited from across the sector. Here the early expression of the need for institutions to differentiate became clear. On the question of degree quality and comparability, some contributors to the review, such as the Association of University Teachers (AUT) (representing staff in the older pre-1992 universities), feared the diminution of the price and social value of HE if it was delivered in FE colleges or even the new, post-1992 universities:

> *The advent of single formulae and the cultural wish of newer universities to look in almost all respects like older ones has created mission drift and a narrowing of perspective. We regret this trend [...] (QSC/CVCP, 1997, p. 12).*

The alternative view was expressed by the National Union of Students' submission:

> *It is vital for the development of higher education that a degree from University X is considered to be of an equal standard to that from University Y.*

> *Nothing could be more detrimental to the future of higher education than if the [Dearing] Committee did not robustly defend this view (QSC/CVCP, 1997, p. 9).*

In opposition, Labour proposed a new Higher Education Quality Agency in the *Lifelong Learning* document and in their own submission to Dearing, which called for a 'proper balance between public accountability and institutional independence' (Labour Party, 1996, p. 24), with a membership drawn from academics, representative trade unions, student representatives and professional and employer bodies. One of its intentions was to give the government advice on the development of a national credit framework and professional accreditation for HE teaching (Labour Party, 1996, p. 25). This seemed designed to straddle the divide, with some encouragement of a Credit Accumulation and Transfer (CAT) system (after all, market choice is the corollary of student-financed HE and demand-led expansion) yet with a quality assurance agency (QAA) proposed which would keep most of the signals of market choice hidden within the institutions. In the event, the incoming Labour government chose not to pursue the more radical suggestion of a CAT system. The concept does however reappear in the context of the 'risk' element of the HERA (2017) – see Chapter 3.

The Dearing Committee's own findings also rejected calls for a fully transferable system based on a national set of standards, preferring to see value in diversity and pluralism:

> *Uniformity of programmes and national curricula, one possible approach to the development of national standards, would deny higher education the vitality, excitement and challenge that comes from institutions consciously pursuing distinctive*

> *purposes, with academics having scope to pursue their own scholarship and enthusiasms in their teaching. The task facing higher education is to reconcile that desirable diversity with achievement of reasonable consistency in standards of awards (NCIHE, Chapter 10, 10.3).*

Dearing thus reflected the much broader range of requirements of the HE system that pertained in the newly unified context. Not only was the sector charged with maintaining excellence on an international scale, it would be expected to demonstrate 'excellence in its diverse purposes' (NCIHE, 1997, 1.4, p. 7). This implied that UK higher education must:

- encourage and enable all students – whether they demonstrate the highest intellectual potential or whether they have struggled to reach the threshold of HE – to achieve beyond their expectations;

- safeguard the rigour of its awards, ensuring that UK qualifications meet the needs of UK students and have standing throughout the world;

- be at the leading edge of world practice in effective learning and teaching; ensure that its support for regional and local communities is at least comparable to that provided by HE in competitor nations;

- be part of the conscience of a democratic society, founded on respect for the rights of the individual and the responsibilities of the individual to society as a whole;

- be explicit and clear in how it goes about its business, be accountable to students and to society, and seek continuously to improve its own performance (NCIHE, 1997, 1.4, pp. 7–8).

These bold aims incorporated the Robbins principle of offering places to all that can benefit, here couched as an expression of the social conscience of a democratic society alongside an emphasis on effective teaching and learning that not only reflects the need to be internationally competitive in standards and quality, but that must meet the ever-changing needs of 'the learning society' (see the following section) – a reflection of the continuing importance of human capital arguments:

> *1.14 Experience suggests that the long-term demand from industry and commerce will be for higher levels of education and training for their present and future workforce. The UK cannot afford to lag behind its competitors in investing in the intellect and skills of its people (NCIHE, 1997, 1.4, p. 8).*

Noting that the UK was falling further behind the United States and Japan in the numbers educated to higher level, the report strongly argued for continuing expansion:

> *1.15 The economic imperative is, therefore, to resume growth. In a 20-year context, participation rates by young people of 40 per cent or beyond have been canvassed by those giving evidence to us. This has already been achieved in Northern Ireland and in Scotland, with participation rates by young people of around 45 per cent. Much of the increase may be among people seeking qualifications below degree level, as in Scotland. Whatever the means of delivery and level of achievement, however, it is clear that growth in participation by traditional young entrants will need to resume. The present cap on continued expansion must be seen as a temporary pause following several years of very fast growth (NCIHE, 1997, section 1.5, pp. 9–10).*

All this naturally implied 'a diverse range of autonomous, well-managed institutions with a commitment to excellence in the achievement of their distinctive missions' (NCIHE, 1997, 1.5, p. 8). This diversity should recognise that 'those [institutions] which already have an established world reputation should be able to retain their distinctive characters: there should be no pressure on them to change their character' (NCIHE, 1997, section 1.6, p. 8). Dearing also sought to balance competition and collaboration between institutions, indeed 'diversity will become the basis for collaboration between complementary institutions to their mutual advantage, and to the advantage of the communities of which they are part' (NCIHE, 1997, section 1.8, p. 8).

This can be seen as endorsing the need for institutions to continue to develop links between 'mission groups', a process already begun among the older established pre-1992 universities. The Russell Group of large research-intensive universities with medical schools, and the 1994 Group of smaller research-intensive pre-1992 universities had both been established in 1994 and, as we have noted above, such institutions (and allies such as the AUT) had sought to differentiate their offer from those of the newer post-1992s and colleges during the Review's consultation phase. The encompassing of 130 institutions within a new regulatory arrangement, following the 1992 Act, created the conditions under which all institutions would be obliged to establish positionality in the marketplace (Fairclough, 1993; Gibbs & Knapp, 2002; McCaig, 2011, 2015, 2018a, 2018b). Such differential positionality – as Dearing recognised – would be based largely on pre-existing strengths:

> *1.6 Institutions of higher education do not and will not fit into simple categories: they do and will*

> *emphasise different elements in their chosen purposes and activities: they are and will be diverse.*
>
> *1.7 Many institutions will see their distinctive contribution in offering first class teaching. They will find innovative and effective ways to extend the opportunity for learning to a larger and broader section of the community. Some institutions will seek to interact creatively with local and regional communities. Some will see a distinctive role in applying the knowledge gained from research to addressing practical problems (NCIHE, 1997, p. 8).*

1.7. EFFICIENCY AND HUMAN CAPITAL MAXIMISATION: THE LEARNING SOCIETY

The 'learning society', the embodiment of 'lifelong learning', was another important theme for Dearing, encapsulating the socially desirable aims of WP and encouraging institutional diversity with the need to maximise human capital in the name of international competitiveness:

> *1.12 The pace of change in the work-place will require people to re-equip themselves, as new knowledge and new skills are needed for economies to compete, survive and prosper. A lifelong career in one organisation will become increasingly the exception. People will need the knowledge and skills to control and manage their own working lives.*
>
> *1.13 This requires a learning society, which embraces both education and training, for people at all levels of achievement, before, during and, for continued personal fulfilment, after working life (NCIHE, 1997, p. 9).*

Both terms had become almost ubiquitous during the 1990s with the opposition Labour Party contributing to what was becoming a consensus which continued into government following the 1997 election (DfEE, 1997; Labour Party, 1996). Internationally there had been a European Year of Lifelong Learning (1996), a World Conference on Lifelong Learning (1997) and in 1998 the Mumbai Declaration on Lifelong Learning, and in UK policy terms these reflected the growing acceptance among policymakers that governments have no other option in a global marketplace but to maximise their human capital. Firms have to be free to respond to changing markets, and employees could not expect job security if they are not multi-skilled and retrainable. The importance of lifelong learning and the learning society within the polity was evidenced by a clutch of documents from a variety of sources throughout the 1990s. These include the Kennedy Report, *Learning Works* (Kennedy, 1997), commissioned by the Further Education Funding Council and published after three years of evidence gathering, and Bob Fryer's National Advisory Group for Continuing Education and Lifelong Learning established after the election in 1997 by David Blunkett, and in response to a suggestion from the Dearing Report (Fryer, 1997).

The underlying reality facing policymakers was that Britain in the 1990s fell below other countries in the number of 25- to 29-year-olds who had A level or the equivalent NVQ level 3. In 1993, only 50% of 25- to 29-year-olds had attained A level or NVQ level 3 compared to 59% for an average of 11 EU states (excluding Italy) (Coffield, 1998). The training deficit in Britain was evidenced by the Labour Force Survey of 1996 which showed that only 15% of employees had had any work-related training in the last month (Labour Force Survey, 1996). The World Competitiveness Report judged Britain at 40th out of

48 countries for 'motivation to retrain', 39th for 'equal opportunities regardless of background' and 35th for 'adequacy of the education system' (World Economic Forum, 1995).

1.8. DEARING, NEW LABOUR AND THE INTRODUCTION OF TUITION FEES

On the subject of fees, the Dearing Review made the case that HE institutions had long been underfunded and that the benefits and costs of HE should be shared. Dearing declared 'a new compact between society, as represented by the Government, students and their families, employers and providing institutions' (NCIHE, 1997, p. 282). More subtly, Dearing used the arguments for expansion (in the name of the nations' human capital) and social justice (the desirability of WP to social groups hitherto under-represented) to offer institutions a *quid pro quo*: they would receive more money, and would be expected to grow their numbers, particularly from such untapped demand:

> *The various beneficiaries of higher education should share its costs and public funding should be distributed equitably so that individuals are not denied access to higher education through lack of financial means (NCIHE, 1997, p. 282).*

From the institutions' point of view, this partial student-financed fee income would help alleviate previous cuts to the unit of resource, although the proposed £1,000 fee (around 25% of the cost of provision) was seen as inadequate. Indeed, the Russell Group had been threatening to charge 'top-up' fees above the basic fee to reflect the higher costs of some of their provision, particularly in relation to medical schools and lab-based sciences, and the prevailing pedagogic mode of small-class tutorials. This debate was to continue until a mechanism for differentiated fees was introduced in the 2004 HE Act. The Dearing Report, for its part, made it clear that new income was unlikely to come from the public purse:

> *The need to supplement public funding has been given sharper focus first by the publicly-stated views of the main national political parties that, notwithstanding the priority they afford to education, higher education could not expect additional public funding, at least in the short-term (NCIHE, 1997, p. 289).*

Dearing reported in July 1997 to a new Labour government, elected only a few months before, which welcomed the emphasis on WP and immediately declared that it would introduce fees as recommended. However, fearing the effect of fees on participation among the poorest, the government decided to introduce a system of fee reductions for those from low residual household incomes(RHI), severely reducing the fee income for institutions. Lobbying in favour of top-up fees was redoubled by older universities and their representatives (e.g. the AUT and the CVCP) (Barr & Crawford, 1997; Crequer, 1997; Thompson, 1997), reflecting pre-election pressure reported by other key policy actors such as NATFHE (McCaig, 2000, p. 265). The debate went beyond the levels of fees: the AUT were concerned about New Labour's adoption of the discourses of lifelong learning, fearing its potential to damage the interests of 'HE as a distinctive activity', concerned not with employability or competitiveness but with the search for 'the truth, the whole truth and nothing but the truth' (McCaig, 2000, p. 266). While diversity remained officially celebrated, the introduction of tuition fees and governmental pressure for socially just expansion (all universities were asked to submit plans on how they would widen participation from 1999) invited equivalent pressure to differentiate the system.

1.9. DIVERSITY INTO THE 2000s

HEFCE set out its official position on sustaining and promoting diversity in HE diversity in a policy statement (HEFCE, 2000, 00/33) and reiterated its mission statement:

Strategic aim is to: 'Maintain and encourage the development of a wide variety of institutions, with a diversity of missions that build upon their local, regional, national and international strengths and are responsive to change, within a financially healthy sector' (HEFCE Strategic Plan 2000-05; HEFCE, 00/22).

But while the language in support of system diversity was largely unchanged from the 1994 founding statement (HEFCE, 1994), the later document introduces some caveats that possibly reflect new thinking in government and the sector:

The promotion of diversity cannot be the sole objective in the development of higher education. Taken in isolation, diversity could always be increased through greater tailoring of programmes or differentiation of institutions to meet the needs and wishes of individual students, employers and others. But such individualisation will tend to increase costs, notably in teaching and administration, by forgoing economies of scale. So diversity has to be balanced against the resources

> *available, from public and private sources (HEFCE, 2000, 00/33, para 13).*

This reminder of the national economic interest juxtaposed against those whose 'needs and aspirations are becoming increasingly varied' as 'participation in higher education gets progressively wider' suggests a new approach to 'the understanding of how higher education can contribute to the economic, social and cultural development of the nation' (HEFCE, 2000, 00/33, para 12):

> *In this sense, diversity of HE provision is not an end in itself. It is a means of securing the best fit with the needs and wishes of stakeholders, both current and future. Diversity is valuable to the extent that it helps to improve that fit. It should develop and expand to keep pace with changing circumstances, and should itself help to shape and raise aspirations and expectations (HEFCE, 2000, 00/33, para 12).*

Diversity is explained and rationalised in terms of the provision of 'choices in curriculum offered; choices of mode pace and place of delivery; choices regarding the physical and intellectual environment available; and choices between a range of different institutional forms and missions'. These were to be facilitated by a diversity of institutions, diversity within and between institutions and 'a capacity for dynamism, responsiveness and change within the sector' (HEFCE, 2000, 00/33, para 14). HEFCE evidenced this diversity in terms of number and type of institutions (including some private) and the number of nontraditional students (part-time, mature) supported. These represent diversity within the system rather than between or within institutions. It is at this stage that limits to diversity are most openly discussed.

> *We need to ask whether there are any boundary tests that should be applied, in terms of forms of diversity which are undesirable. We see merit in the argument of one commentator that institutional diversity should be defined as 'defensible difference'. Autonomous institutions should pursue diversity but be prepared to justify their actions (HEFCE, 2000, 00/33, para 22).*

Here once again the question of quality — noted above in relation to the debates around Dearing — come back into play, this time overtly linked to the expansion of the sector and, by definition, widened access:

> *We believe that some measure of consistency is required in respect of quality and standards. It was traditionally a presumption of British higher education that an HE qualification should denote a broadly comparable level of achievement irrespective of the institution at which it was obtained. There is debate about how far that presumption retains any validity, given the rapid expansion of the past 15 years, the variation in students' abilities and aptitudes, and differences in institutions' circumstances, endowments and missions. Some commentators have argued against the presumption of comparability altogether, advocating a more purely market-based system (HEFCE, 2000, 00/33, para 24).*

This was raised but, in keeping with other themes identified in this study, not followed through at this point. HEFCE made it clear that among the ways to ensure the maintenance of standards and the economic interest, it favoured institutional mergers in the context of the limits to institutions' autonomy when it came to diversifying provision:

> *We will not allocate additional funds to institutions just so that they can remain independent, if that additional funding cannot also be justified by reference to the quality, cost and distinctiveness of their provision. Institutional mergers between higher education institutions continue to take place. Some people have taken this as evidence of diminishing diversity. But the maintenance of a given number of separate institutions is not a goal in its own right if it requires extra funding without achieving a better fit with stakeholders' needs.*
>
> *Where an institution concludes that it is not able to sustain financial viability and academic health on standard funding, we do not believe it would be appropriate to allocate additional funding to avert merger at any cost (HEFCE, 2000, 00/33, paras 27 and 28).*

While HEFCE was clearly minded to indicate the limits to the encouragement of a diversity of provision by institutions, it also used the policy statement to reassert its systemic support for aspects of government policy. These were in three main areas: support for institutions that recruited a larger than average number of WP students (i.e. from under-represented groups) in the form of student funding premia; additional student numbers, for example where institutions wished to expand sub-degree numbers; and an invitation to around 40 private providers (whose programmes were designated to enable their students to claim support towards payment of fees) to apply to enter the HE sector and thereby become eligible for direct HEFCE funding, in order to help 'enrich the institutional diversity of the sector' (HEFCE, 2000, 00/33, para 43).

1.10. SUMMARY

This chapter has covered the first two main stages of marketisation, conceptualised as discursive sets of arguments for reform (summarised in **Tables 1.1 and 1.2**). On the face of it, they could appear unrelated: arguments for greater accountability and efficiency in public spending (Jarrett and Croham) were unremarkable examples of New Public Management responses to the political desire to simultaneously reduce the size of the state and meet the economic need to develop the nation's human capital by expanding its high-skills base. Yet, the desire to divest the state of responsibility for further and HE (the 1988 Education Reform Act and the 1992 Further and Higher Education Act) created a managed market with perhaps unintended consequences for institutions, now expected to find their own niche, urging them to diversify alternative income streams and offer innovative provision. That these newly empowered institutions would feel the need to differentiate to the extent that their own organisational imperatives would drive the next stages of marketisation would have seemed unlikely in 1992.

Table 1.1. Stage Analysis Table 'Accountability and Efficiency'.

Stage 1: Efficiency and Accountability	Centralisation vs Autonomy	Efficiency in Public Services	Funding Mode (Block or Service Provider by Unit)	New Sources of Income	Human Capital Arguments	Diversity as a Good	Quality
Jarratt (1985) and Croham (1987) reports 1987 Bill	Business influence on UFC. End of academic tenure. Removal of LA control – DfES overall oversight	Business on institutional and UFC boards. Freedom to develop new programmes	Block grant. Need to move to a service provider model	Academic capitalism encouraged – don't rely solely on state block grants	Efficiency driven by need to grow the system	n/a	Assumed
1988 Education Reform Act	Polytechnics Funding Council with business on board	Polytechnics Funding Council with	Service provision – state as	Universities and Polytechnics to	Local and regional labour markets	Assumed	Assumed

1992 Further and Higher Education Act	End of the binary divide – founding councils merged into HEFCE (HEFCW, SHEFC) More autonomy for new universities and FE sector freed from LA control (incorporation)	business on board Unit costs lowered – leading to growth Growth expected to continue at lower unit cost	customer, institutions as providers Service provision – state as customer, institutions as providers	develop as regional power bases New universities (post-1992s) take on more regional labour market role Free to develop curriculum to meet local/regional demand	Local and regional labour markets International competitiveness	Diversity of student body encouraged	Rejects fears of diluted quality in newly expanded sector

Table 1.2. Stage Analysis Table 'Diversity as a Good'.

| Stage 2: Diversity and Human Capital | Arguments Employed/Developed |||||||
	Centralisation vs Autonomy	Efficiency in Public Services	Funding Mode (Block or Service Provider by Unit)	New Sources of Income	Human Capital Arguments	Diversity as a Good	Quality
Dearing Report and New Labour government (1997)	Dearing recommends: QAA; Credit Accumulation and Transfer system WP encouraged; funded by the state	Growth expected to continue, more fee-income released for institutions	Dearing: fees to be paid by students at 25% of cost of degrees, keep maintenance grants Labour government: £1,000 fees (with exemptions for poorest) but remove grants	Develop new vocational curricula in response to needs of labour market Labour launched foundation degrees to help achieve 50% young participation target	Lifelong learning promoted as a good	D. WP encouraged Labour introduce requirements from HEIs to say what they are doing to widen participation Labour introduces state-funded WP programmes	Dearing rejects overtly market solutions on quality. Suggests QAA to ensure quality is assured across the sector. Labour adopts

The Genesis of Market Reforms

HEFCE statements (1994; 2000)	Control over student numbers Directive about WP as a government priority – some funding incentives for WP	Control over student numbers; allocations based on previous performance	HEFCE 2000 additional funding for WP students to reflect cost of teaching	HEFCE 2000 diversity must be justified by demand	Assumed	HEFCE 1994 statement encouraged and celebrates diversity of mission and student body; HEFCE 2000 diversity must be justified by demand and efficiency	Assumed not to be an issue

CHAPTER 2

FROM DIVERSITY TO DIFFERENTIATION: THE COMING OF THE MARKET

The third stage of marketisation, from around 2000 to 2010, can be seen as the beginnings of the era of system differentiation with the encouragement in legislation of variable fees and variable student support packages. Legislation and other governmental activity, including the 2003 White Paper *The Future of Higher Education* (DfES, 2003), reports by the Social Mobility Commission (SMC, 2009), the *Higher Ambitions* White Paper (DBIS, 2009) and the ensuing Browne Review of student finance (2010), encouraged individualisation and difference in positionality as institutions sought a 'place' in the market. Beyond 'official policy', other prerequisites of a functioning market differentiation were falling into place. Institutional league tables first emerged in 2005 to feed and reflect market positionality and from this period we can trace the emergence of a vertical differentiation of institutions (Archer, 2007) which has rapidly become the single metric by which institutions are judged.

The fourth stage (2010–2015) more overtly celebrates 'competitive differentiation', with a White Paper *Students at the Heart of the System* that incentivises the concentration of high attainers ('bright young people' in the words of a senior member of the Coalition government) at the 'best universities' and the devil, apparently, encouraged to take the hindmost with new cheaper 'challenger' providers invited to market.

2.1. THE 2003 WHITE PAPER AND HIGHER EDUCATION ACT 2004

As explored in the first chapter, the period between 1992 and the early 2000s can be characterised as a period in which system diversity was encouraged and celebrated in the wake of the unification of the HE sector after 1992 (Further and Higher Education Act, HMSO, 1992). However, a large part of the context of the 2003 White Paper and ensuing 2004 Act was dealing with the rise in tuition fees. Basic fees of £1,000 per year of study (estimated to be around 25% of the actual costs) for students from families above a RHI cut-off were introduced in 1998 to provide institutions with much-needed additional income. However, due to the high numbers of students who were at least partly exempt, insufficient money was considered to be making its way to institutions (Barr & Crawford, 1997). Therefore, pressure was immediately placed on the Labour government to renege on its promise not to introduce 'top up' or 'variable' fees, a key pledge that enabled the National Union of Students and the internal Labour Students caucus to support the £1,000 fees at the 1995 and 1996 Labour Party conferences (McCaig, 2000, p. 278). Variable fees thereafter become a marker of competitive differentiation (in theory at least), reflecting a belief that some HE delivered by some HE institutions was inherently more valuable than that offered elsewhere in the system, would be more attractive to highly qualified applicants and thus would justify a higher fee. The 2003 White Paper set out to establish such a market.

2.2. THE ARGUMENT FOR REFORM: VARIABLE TUITION FEES

Evoking the need to expand the system for human capital reasons, Secretary of State for Education and Skills Charles Clarke introduced the need to reform student finance, given that the principle of self-funded HE had been settled, declaring that 'while the Government will continue to pay most of the cost involved in studying for a degree, it is also reasonable to ask students to contribute to this':

> *Our national ability to master that process of change and not be ground down by it depends critically upon our universities. Our future success depends upon mobilizing even more effectively the imagination, creativity, skills and talents of all our people. And it depends on using that knowledge and understanding to build economic strength and social harmony (DFES, 2003, Foreword).*

Of equal importance was the need to widen participation, something that could be threatened by higher tuition fee costs:

> *[...] we need to make sure that no student is put off from going into higher education because they cannot afford the cost of studying while they are at university. And those who come from the poorest backgrounds should get extra support. This White*

> *Paper declares our intention to take the tough decisions on higher education, to deal with student finance for the long term, to open up access to our universities, and to allow them to compete with the best (DFES, 2003, Foreword).*

Measures were introduced to protect and encourage widening participation (WP). Means-tested maintenance grants (abolished by the Labour government in 1998) were to be reintroduced, along with the abolition of upfront fees to be replaced by an income-contingent repayment system for graduates. Institutions would have to agree an 'Access Agreement to improve access for disadvantaged students, before they are able to increase the level of fee they ask students to pay'. Such agreements would be regulated by the OFFA in order to 'to promote wider access and to ensure that admissions procedures are fair, professional and transparent' (DfES, 2003, Executive Summary).

The management of a system designed to increase funding for institutions whilst protecting wider access to HE was promoted as the main driver for reform. Diversity remained celebrated and quality was not assumed to be threatened either in terms of international competiveness or within the system:

> *[...] the rate of return from higher education in the UK is higher than in any other OECD country. Our non-completion rate for first degrees remains just 17 per cent, which is almost the lowest in the OECD (DfES, 2003, para 1.7).*

> *Our system has successfully transformed itself from an elite system – in which, in 1962, only around 6 per cent those under 21 participated – to one where in England around 43 per cent of those aged between 18 and 30 go to university. Despite the rise*

> *in the numbers participating in higher education, the average salary premium has not declined over time and remains the highest in the OECD. It is not the case that 'more means worse' (DfES, 2003, para 1.9).*

However, while system diversity was celebrated, WP encouraged and the introduction of variable fees rationalised, the White Paper for the first time envisaged a market-like scenario in which institutions were encouraged to differentiate themselves. This would have important repercussions for the way that WP developed (McCaig & Adnett, 2009) which will be explored more fully in Chapter 3 of this volume.

The White Paper linked diversity to the need to encourage institutions to differentiate their offer: this 'needs to be acknowledged and celebrated, with institutions both openly identifying and playing to their strengths' (DfES, 2003, para 1.38). Highlighting the ways in which HEFCE, as primary funder of research and allocator of student numbers, has always shaped the sector, the White Paper provided a 'radical picture of a freer future' for institutions in the form of variable fees:

> *Government will continue to be the principal funder of higher education, but we need to move to a funding regime which enables each institution to choose its mission and the funding streams necessary to support it, and to make sure that our system recognises and celebrates different missions properly (DfES, 2003, para 1.39).*

It would remain the 'duty of government to make sure that the transition is managed carefully and sensibly so that change is not destabilising'. Government, it was believed 'has to retain a role because it is the only body that can balance competing interests between the different stakeholders' (DfES, 2003, para 1.43). Here we can see most clearly the radical departure from the earlier encouragement and celebration of diversity for its own sake to a position in which differentiation is encouraged. Institutions were to be free to vary provision (in response to student demand), set their own tuition fees (up to the new ceiling of £3,000) and choose their approaches to WP and ensuring fair access to HE (with protection for the poorest and other under-represented groups). Whereas initially market thinking was applied in terms of accountability and efficiency in the 1980s, the diversification of income streams and encouragement of institutional diversity where it existed across the newly unified system after 1992, now marketisation was encouraged within the closed system in the form of differentiation.

What were to be the drivers of market differentiation in this new landscape? Institutions would need to demonstrate to applicants that they were choosing the best or most appropriate courses and institutions to meet their demands. This would be facilitated by better market signalling mechanisms:

> *To become intelligent customers of an increasingly diverse provision, and to meet their own increasing diverse needs, students need accessible information. We will ensure that the views of students themselves are published in a national annual survey available for the first time in Autumn 2003, which will explicitly cover teaching quality (DfES, 2003, para 4.2).*

Applicant choice and student views would thus drive up quality, and students' consumer rights would be protected by an independent adjudicator in the case of poor provision (DfES, 2003, para 4.12). Teaching quality was evoked, but mainly in the context of encouraging 'teaching-only' institutions to enhance the diversity of the system:

> *At present, the 'University' title is reserved for institutions that have the power to award both taught degrees, and research degrees. The right to award research degrees requires that the institution demonstrate its strength in research. This situation is at odds with our belief that institutions should play to diverse strengths, and that excellent teaching is, in itself, a core mission for a university [...] It is clear that good scholarship, in the sense of remaining aware of the latest research and thinking within a subject, is essential for good teaching, but not that it is necessary to be active in cutting-edge research to be an excellent teacher (DfES, 2003, para 4.31).*

There was a move designed to encourage institutions to engage in directly funded HEFCE provision of foundation degrees and other sub-degree qualifications:

> *We propose to change the system, so that the University title is awarded on the basis of taught degree awarding powers, student numbers, and the range of subjects offered. This will send an important signal about the importance of teaching, and about the benefits for some institutions of focusing their efforts on teaching well.*

> *At the same time, we will examine and modernise the criteria for degree-awarding powers to reflect the increasing diversity of higher education. The current system does not sufficiently reflect factors such as new virtual learning models, or the legitimate roles of those outside the university sector in providing*

> *high quality higher education learning. But there will be no relaxation of the high standards that have to be reached before taught degree awarding powers are granted (DfES, 2003, para 4.34).*

This re-evocation of the importance of standards can be seen as an important demarcation of the 2003 Act in relation to the 2017 Higher Education and Research Act. The latter document takes differentiation further by introducing the element of risk through the presence of competition – arguably the final element of a fully functioning market in HE and one that takes it beyond the confines of a 'system'. Not only will institutions risk losing students to competitors if undercut by price or perceived quality, they will have to insure against risk by entering into partnership agreements with local competitors guaranteeing that students will not lose out (in financial or economic terms). Moreover, institutions would face the risk of closure by the withdrawal of the Secretary of State's commitment to prevent failure.

The 2003 White Paper fits neatly into our definition of neoliberalism by attempting to shape the supply and demand factors in the system in the national interest – specifically in relation to foundation degrees. In a section entitled 'Expanding higher education to meet our needs' the document cited recent research which showed that education remained highly likely to expand economic growth 'by stimulating more effective use of resources, and more physical capital investment and technology adoption' (DfES, 2003, para 5.3). However, the state retained the right to shape the system:

> *But we do not believe that expansion should mean 'more of the same'. There is a danger of higher education becoming an automatic step in the chain*

> *of education – almost a third stage of compulsory schooling. We do not favour expansion on the single template of the traditional three year honours degree (DfES, 2003, para 5.8).*

This encouragement for alternative HE routes and trajectories was used to justify the deregulation of tuition fees: institutions would be provided with the 'flexibility to position their programmes in accordance with the costs of and perceived returns to particular qualifications. Foundation degrees are likely to be priced competitively in such a market' (DfES, 2003, para 5.15).

The final section of the White Paper detailed the shift from upfront tuition fees to the new Graduate Contribution Scheme:

> *The principle that it is right for students to make a contribution to the costs of their course was established by Lord Dearing in 1997. It is now generally accepted, and raises £450 million a year. But universities have asked us to consider whether students might be asked to contribute more to the cost of their education (DfES, 2003, para 7.20).*

The mechanism of repayment was clearly driven by the need for more income, as we can see by the positioning of the rationale for a graduate contribution scheme, itself presented as a means by which institutions can further free themselves from the yoke of government funding:

> *Given these benefits to an individual from the investment in a university education, the government has decided that it is fair to allow universities, if they so determine, to ask students to make an increased contribution – as they do in Australia, New*

> *Zealand, Canada and the United States. We believe that this will also have the benefit of enhancing the independence of universities by making them less reliant on government funding (DfES, 2003, para 7.22).*

The White Paper can thus be seen as a document that simultaneously responds to institutional pressure for more direct income and presents HEIs with the freedom to reposition themselves, should they wish to do so, in a market distribution of institutions. Of course, as with the following 2011 White Paper *Students at the Heart of the System*, the various incentives (freedom to treble tuition fees; freedom of approach to widen participation; freedom to expand into new provision such as foundation degrees; encouragement of teaching-only institutions) would appeal to different types of institutions, further driving differentiation within the system.

Measures of student satisfaction were a key component driving choice in the system, but they would not be alone in providing applicants with a better understanding of the value of an institution's provision. Alongside the caveat that institutions that are 'given the freedom to raise higher contributions from students' only on condition that they have 'an Access Agreement in place' to safeguard access (DfES, 2003, para 7.23), an open fee market would mean that:

> *[...] institutions will be able to reap rewards for offering courses that serve students well. It will make student choice a much more powerful force, and help choice drive quality (DfES, 2003, para 7.28).*

The OFFA was charged with not only ensuring that institutions acted to safeguard widening access, but was now empowered also to regulate financial support:

> *Institutions are required to use some of the money raised through tuition fees to provide bursaries or other financial support for students from under-represented groups, or to fund outreach activities to encourage more applications from under-represented groups. An access agreement will provide the details of bursary support and outreach work (OFFA, 2005, 16).*

The amount or proportion of additional fee income to be spent was not prescribed, but as noted above:

> *Institutions whose record suggests that they have further to go in attracting a wider range of applications will be expected to be more ambitious in their access agreement (OFFA, 2005, 17).*

The 2003 White Paper and 2004 HE Act thus introduced a price differential that was assumed to reflect the quality of provision and by extension student type, given the earlier assertion that foundation degrees were 'likely to be priced competitively in such a market' (DfES, 2003, 2.15). A price-quality distribution in the form of a 'dual pricing' mechanism (where the UCAS tariff requirements mirrored the tuition fee demanded) coupled with the variable financial support packages (above a minimum £300 per year) introduced in the 2004 Higher Education Act (Section 33 F2) created the conditions for a differentiated market. This represents a qualitative difference from the earlier landscape of celebrated diversity (HEFCE, 1994, 2000 00/22; 00/33) described in

Chapter 1. With all the factors in place, why did a market not emerge?

2.3. THE LIMITATIONS OF THE 2004 HE ACT: DIFFERENTIATION WITHOUT COMPETITION

While many commentators such as Harrison (2011) noted that the White Paper and Act were clearly designed to create a financial market in places, in the event, fee variation never materialised (one institution set fees at £2,000 per year initially, but abandoned this after two academic years). It was also noted that 'while there was variation in bursaries it was a weak signal that didn't lead to any applicant behaviour change' (Harrison, 2011, p. 455) due to the difficulties applicants had in deciding which institutions offered the better financial support (McCaig, 2011a, 2011b; McCaig & Adnett, 2009). This was unsurprising given that government and the sector ignored advice to introduce a national bursary scheme that would have reduced the confusion experienced by consumers (see Callendar, 2009; Chester & Bekhradnia, 2008). Institutions were instead encouraged to use WP resources (a proportion of additional fee income derived from the variable tuition fees) to reshape specific patterns of recruitment.

In the event, many of the older (pre-1992) institutions chose to apply the requirement to offer bursary support to students by opting for bursaries based on merit, not needs, offered on top of the basic mandatory bursary, thereby creating a bursary/support market grounded on their own recruitment patterns and needs. Discretionary, targeted support of this nature added layers of complexity to the bursary market which applicants were already struggling to negotiate. In theory, of course, a fully functioning market with perfect information would clear applicants and places, with those most in need of additional support able to access that support; however, due to the variability in bursary/support regimes, the English HE market has never been able to clear in such a straightforward way.

The main restriction on the ability of access agreements to impact on access to HE is the inability of OFFA — or any other agency of the state — to interfere with the autonomy of institutions when it comes to admissions. The recommendations of the Schwartz Review into admissions to HE (*Fair Admissions to Higher Education: Recommendations for Good Practice*) (Admissions to Higher Education Steering Group, 2004) were that admissions systems should be transparent; select students that are able to complete their courses based upon achievements and potential; use assessment methods that are reliable and valid; minimise barriers to applicants; be professional; and be underpinned by appropriate institutional structures and processes (Adnett, McCaig, Bowers-Brown, & Slack, 2011, p. 13). However, the report also remarks:

> *the terms 'fairness', 'fair admissions' and 'fair access' have figured prominently in recent debates about higher education admissions, [but] as McCaig and Adnett (2009) point out, they remain undefined by policy makers. Indeed, OFFA has effectively condoned a system in which each institution unilaterally sets its own criteria for the desired composition of its student intake (Adnett et al., 2011, p. 13).*

So while the 2003 White Paper, the 2004 Act and ensuing OFFA guidance to institutions (OFFA, 2005) all provided the conditions for a differentiated HE market that would constitute a qualitative step away from the celebration of diversity in the earlier period, such a market failed to materialise. The main driver of the reforms was the need to justify a tuition fee rise and at the same time further the process of shifting the burden of tuition costs from the state to the individual. The secondary purpose was to provide institutions with incentives to both grow and widen participation, and even to encourage new providers to the market. The key was to make it easier for applicants (now referred to as 'consumers') to differentiate between the 130 HE institutions (roughly 110 universities and another 20 specialist institutions) in the system that had consolidated in the 1990s. Market signals were established, but it would take the widespread adoption of league tables published by the *Times Higher Education Supplement* and *The Guardian* newspapers to visualise the differentiated distribution of the sector. These were as reliant on research funding metrics as any indicators of actual teaching quality, and soon became regularly used by employers, careers advisors and the media to reinforce the notion of a hierarchical system. This replaced the long-celebrated 'horizontal' differentiation between modes of learning with a 'vertically' differentiated system akin to a price list, discussed further in Chapter 3 of this volume. However, despite the creation of a complex apparatus for a market differential to emerge, no actual market emerged; all institutions had, within two academic years, begun to charge the new maximum fee as demand for HE remained unsatisfied. It soon emerged that while there was a variable market in financial bursaries, it had no impact on patterns of recruitment (McCaig & Adnett, 2009). Perhaps the more pertinent question is why government pursued marketisation through differentiation?

2.4. THE LONG ROAD FROM DIFFERENTIATION TO COMPETITION

In the absence of price competition between institutions and with the market-like positionality of access statements and bursary levels largely obscured from applicants, the fullest expression of a marketised system seemed to have stalled at the point of differentiation. League tables allowed applicants to see that some institutions were rated more highly than others, but system-wide growth (with demand still exceeding supply) and an effective 'price indicator' of UCAS entry tariff points reduced the need for actual competitive behaviour among differentiated institutions. However, government ministers were aware of pressure from within the sector to raise tuition fees once again by 2009 (the Labour government invited Lord Browne of Madingley, a former BP executive, to lead another review of the student finance system) and launched a White Paper *Higher Ambitions: the future of Universities in a knowledge economy* (DBIS, 2009). This document was the first major policy statement issued by the new Department for Business, Innovation and Skills and was aggressive not only in its reiteration of the need for providers to pursue efficiencies and seek other funding streams; institutions also had to diversify provision and attend to the need for informed choice among consumers:

> *Universities already need to be rigorous in withdrawing from activities of lower priority and value, so that they can invest more in higher priority programmes. That will need to intensify. By requiring course content and outcomes to be more transparent, students and employers will be enabled to make informed choices that increase competition between institutions. No student should ever be*

> *misled into believing that a course will deliver employment outcomes that it will not.*
>
> *[...] it is necessary to look afresh at the contribution who benefit from higher education — taxpayers, students, and the private sector. Following the launch of these proposals, the Government will commission an independent review into this question (DBIS, 2009, Foreword by Secretary of State for Business, Innovation and Skills, the Lord Mandelson, p. 4).*

Demand, evoked in the context of the need for the system to move away from the traditional three-year full-time degree, would have to be met by a newly dynamic system. However, this market would also be firmly couched in the language of human capital and the role of the state in system-shaping:

> *However, the next phase of expansion in higher education will hinge on providing opportunities for different types of people to study in a wider range of ways than in the past.*
>
> *[...]*
>
> *We will bring together universities, employers, HEFCE and the UK Commission for Employment and Skills (UKCES) to identify and tackle specific areas where university supply is not meeting demand for key skills, and will expect all universities to describe how they enhance students' employability (DBIS, 2009, Foreword by Secretary of State for Business, Innovation and Skills, the Lord Mandelson, p. 9).*

Much of the 2009 White Paper prefigured the language of the 2011 White Paper *Students at the Heart of the System* (introduced by the Conservative-led Coalition elected in 2010) illustrating the cross-party consensus around the role of markets in HE. For example, all institutions were to publish a standard set of information, outlining what students could expect in terms of the nature and quality of provision:

> *This should set out how and what students will learn, what that knowledge will qualify them to do, whether they will have access to external expertise or experience, how much direct contact there will be with academic staff, what their own study responsibilities will be, what facilities they will have access to, and any opportunities for international experience. It should also offer information about what students on individual courses have done after graduation. The Unistats website [set up in 2007] will continue to bring together information in a comparable way so that students can make well-informed informed choices, based on an understanding of the nature of the teaching programme they can expect, and the long-term employment prospects it offers (DBIS, 2009, Foreword by Secretary of State for Business, Innovation and Skills, the Lord Mandelson, p. 12).*

However, the document also illustrated important aspects of discontinuity. Labour envisaged a continuing role for the regime of Regional Development Agencies to 'provide capital for university schemes that they judge to be of high economic value to the locality and region' (ibid, p. 14) even while it noted the ongoing effects of the 2008 economic crisis which meant that 'growth based so heavily on state funding cannot continue and this confronts government and universities with a series of challenges [...]' (DBIS, 2009, Foreword by Secretary of State for Business, Innovation and Skills, the Lord Mandelson, p. 21) and in the same year the government capped student numbers.

Linking the need for greater competition and differentiation with the new economic realities meant that market positionality would have to be to the fore:

> *Sustaining a diversity of excellence through a period of increased competition and public spending constraint will require each institution to develop its own distinctive mission, and for funding to be focused on investing in and nurturing excellence. Universities may need to withdraw from activities in which they cannot achieve excellence in order to focus on the areas where they can (DBIS, 2009, Foreword by Secretary of State for Business, Innovation and Skills, the Lord Mandelson, p. 22).*

Diversity in these terms meant that institutions should divest themselves of provision in poorly performing segments of the market, either in terms of low demand for these programmes or less remunerative outcomes for their graduates. Instead, institutions should be expanding in other areas of provision that were more likely to engender higher quality applicants (as measured by the UCAS tariff requirements) and thus better graduate outcomes as measured by the Destination of Leavers survey. An institution's distinctive mission, by this definition, should be more narrowly focused than the traditional university model that would encompass all the major disciplines. The discourses around diversity and differentiation, often seen as two sides of the same coin, are here more starkly contrasted: whereas diversity implies broadening and opening out to encourage new ways of being, learning and thinking, differentiation in the DBIS mindset implies an aggressive repositioning designed to maximise business opportunities.

The state would still have a strategic steering role, of course, if the resources provided were to achieve public policy goals (DBIS, 2009, Foreword by Secretary of State for Business, Innovation and Skills, the Lord Mandelson, p. 22). This latter statement could be interpreted as prefiguring the Browne Review's conclusions and the incoming government's decision to retain direct funding for science, technology, engineering and mathematics (STEM) even while the full cost of all other courses would thereafter be met by graduates. Browne went much further in recommending further freedoms for institutions, not only in fee-setting but also in the ways that they should approach WP; they were to be freed from the need to consider system-wide concerns and the need to provide mandatory bursaries to the poorest students (Browne, 2010, p. 38). In the event, the new government rejected the Browne Review's free-market emphasis on system growth (Browne recommended a 10% increase in places) and tuition fees, due the ramifications for public expenditure in a period of post-crash austerity. However, it did sanction the discontinuation of state expenditure on WP in the form of Aimhigher and Lifelong Learning Network partnerships and the abolition of OFFA-regulated bursaries. This would free up institutions to target support where they saw fit.

Browne reported to the new Coalition government and within months, new tuition fee levels were put before Parliament. The basic fee was to rise to £6,000 (from £1,000) and the new variable fee was set up to a maximum of £9,000 per year of study (from £3,000). While this created a predictable level of political disquiet and public protest, the retention of a fee cap lower than that recommended by Browne who envisaged a 'soft-cap of around £12,000' (Browne, 2010, p. 37) was clearly driven by the need to maintain control of the public expenditure outcomes, given that many graduates would never be able to repay the full amount. Browne outlined the ramifications for public expenditure in his Foreword to the report:

> *We estimate that only the top 40% of earners on average will pay back all the charges paid on their behalf by the Government upfront; and the 20% of lowest earners will pay less than today (Browne, 2010, Foreword).*

This prediction of the proportion of graduates fully repaying their fee loans proved to be close to that estimated by government after Parliament voted to accept the new higher fee levels in November 2010, with the new fee and repayment system to come into place in 2012–2013. An important part of government's policy thinking was the financial modelling that estimated the system to be affordable if the average fee set by institutions was to be around £7,500. This assumed a price distribution to (roughly) match the UCAS tariff distribution of institutions, with an expectation that only the 'best' institutions would charge the maximum while other institutions would be forced to compete on price, i.e., set fees lower than £7,500, referred to as a 'dual-price mechanism' in Bowl et al. 2018. In the event, average fees for 2012–2013 settled around £8,365, far closer to the maximum fee than anticipated, presaging an affordability crisis to go with a future graduate debt crisis. As much as anything else, the need to deal with higher-than-anticipated tuition fees was to drive the next major policy document, the White Paper *Students at the Heart of the System* (DBIS, 2011).

2.5. THE FOURTH STAGE: STUDENT NUMBER CONTROLS AND MARKET-INCENTIVISED DIFFERENTIATION

While on one level we could view the fees debate since their introduction and steady increase from 1998 to 2010 as part of the overall sweep of marketisation, many of the elements of marketisation and differentiation were present prior to 1998. The perceived need for greater accountability and efficiency in the publicly funded system, the human capital rationale for system growth and a national steering of provision were as present in the Croham Committee's report as in *The Future of Higher Education* (DfES, 2003), *Higher Ambitions* (DBIS, 2009) and *Students at the Heart of the System* (DBIS, 2011). However, while these elements remained, diversity was now re-conceptualised as differentiation and that had to be encouraged by competition for student places if the financial support system was to persist. To that extent, the presence of fees as a concomitant to system growth and widened participation can be seen as a critical driver of reforms since 1998.

The 2011 document announced reforms designed to:

> *deliver a more responsive higher education sector in which funding follows the decisions of learners and successful institutions are freed to thrive; in which there is a new focus on the student experience and the quality of teaching and in which further education colleges and other alternative providers are encouraged to offer a diverse range of higher education provision.*
>
> *The overall goal is higher education that is more responsive to student choice, that provides a better student experience and that helps improve social*

> *mobility (DBIS, 2011, Executive Summary, paras 23−24).*

The centrepiece of the White Paper was a system of SNCs directly addressing the lack of a fee distribution, couched — as ever — in greater freedom of movement for institutions:

> *We will tackle the micro-management that has been imposed on the higher education sector in recent years and which has held institutions back from responding to student demand. We must move away from a world in which the number of students allocated to each university is determined in Whitehall. But universities will be under competitive pressure to provide better quality and lower cost (DBIS, 2011, Executive Summary, para 5).*

The SNC regime was to take two forms, together making 85,000 student places 'contestable' between institutions by dividing allocations into 'core' and 'margin'. First, 'we will allow unconstrained recruitment of the roughly 65,000 high achieving students, scoring the equivalent of AAB or above at A-Level' (DBIS, 2011, Executive Summary, para 8). This would enable successful institutions to grow their proportion of high attaining students (and thus their margin), but at the expense of those with lower entry qualifications (the shrinking core), because the overall student number allocation would remain the same for each institution. Thus, the overall 'quality' profile of such institutions could be consolidated, further differentiating them from less successful institutions and acting as an important market signal to consumers. The second element was the creation of a:

> *flexible margin of about 20,000 places to reward universities and colleges who combine good quality*

> *with value for money and whose average tuition charge [...] is at or below £7,500 per year (DBIS, 2011, Executive Summary, para 8).*

This was a clear signal to institutions that could not compete on quality (in other words that would potentially lose 'high achieving' AAB+ students to other institutions) that they should compete downwards on price. Twenty-three lower-ranking HEIs bid for these margin numbers in the second year of the SNC regime, thus reducing their average fees. Further education colleges which had often acted as 'franchise partners' of universities, delivering part or all of degree and sub-degree programmes, and alternative providers, with lower cost bases than universities, were encouraged to bid directly for these places in competition with existing HEIs. Other passages of the White Paper discussed the kind of regulatory reform that would make it easier for alternative providers to enter the market more competitively, with their own degree-awarding powers (DAP) and able to attain University Title (UT). However, these reforms would require legislation which, as the Minister of Universities David Willets noted in a speech six months prior to the publication of the White Paper, would not happen in time for the introduction of the new market incentives (David Willetts MP, DBIS, October 2010).

Reiterating the need for institutions to diversify their income streams, the White Paper noted that places could be created outside of the SNC where sponsored by employers and charities but 'provided they do not create a cost liability for Government' (David Willetts MP, DBIS, October 2010, para 8). The need to reduce public spending on HE, easily evoked in the wider hegemonic austerity discourse of the period after 2008, could be portrayed as 'common sense' while at the same time used to further ideological ends, the enhancement of consumer choice and social mobility:

> *Our reforms tackle three challenges. First, putting higher education on a sustainable footing. We inherited the largest budget deficit in post-war history, requiring spending cuts across government. By shifting public spending away from teaching grants and towards repayable tuition loans, we have ensured that higher education receives the funding it needs even as substantial savings are made to public expenditure. Second, institutions must deliver a better student experience; improving teaching, assessment, feedback and preparation for the world of work. Third, they must take more responsibility for increasing social mobility (DBIS, 2011, Executive Summary, para 3).*

The economic recession enabled government to display a degree of reluctance, even while many commentators (McCaig & Taylor, 2015; Taylor & McCaig, 2014) regarded these conditions as a convenient scapegoat, along with the Labour government believed to have presided over the 2008 crash, which obliged market dirigisme:

> *It fell to the Coalition to receive the report by the Independent Review of Higher Education Funding and Student Finance (the 'Browne Review'), which was established by the previous Government. We were given the report in an environment when public funding had to be reduced and we accepted the main thrust – that the beneficiaries of higher education would need to make a larger contribution towards its costs (DBIS, 2011, Executive Summary, para 4).*

Adopting the 'hair shirt' of unpopularity, the authors of the White Paper combined an acknowledgement of inevitability with a promise to retain fairness and to actually increase income for institutions:

> *We inherited an enormous deficit which required difficult decisions. The changes to student finance have been controversial. We could have reduced student numbers or investment per student or introduced a less progressive graduate repayment mechanism. But these would all have been unfair to students, higher education institutions and the country. Instead our proposals for graduate contributions ensure good universities will be well funded for the long term. We estimate there will be a cash increase in funding for higher education of around ten per cent by 2014–15 but more of the expenditure will eventually be recouped from graduates' contributions, improving the student experience (DBIS, 2011, Executive Summary, para 4).*

Having dispensed with the 'why' of reform, the argument turned to the mechanism. In a climate when Ministers were openly anticipating a reduction in student numbers and the first real contraction of the system since the 1970s, consumer choice would be critical (Cable, 2010).

2.6. CHOICE AS THE NEW FRONTIER

Applicants had been exhorted and encouraged to use their consumer power in several phases since 2004, of course, to little avail. From academic year 2012–13, price variation would make it clearer to applicants that if they did not achieve the attainment level required for the 'best' institutions (and thus remunerative careers), they should exercise financial power by choosing to attend a lower-priced institution:

> *The changes we are making to higher education funding will in turn drive a more responsive system. To be successful, institutions will have to appeal to prospective students and be respected by employers. Putting financial power into the hands of learners makes student choice meaningful (DBIS, 2011, Executive Summary, para 6).*

The key was to be more informative for applicants:

> *We will radically improve and expand the information available to prospective students, making available much more information about individual courses at individual institutions and graduate employment prospects. We are asking UCAS and higher education institutions to make available, course by course, new data showing the type and subjects of the actual qualifications held by previously successful applicants. We will ask the main organisations that hold student data to make detailed data available publicly, including on employment and earnings outcomes, so it can be analysed and presented by private organisations in a variety of formats to meet the needs of students, their parents and other advisors (DBIS, 2011, Executive Summary, para 11).*

In order to facilitate choice-driven competition, a series of regulatory changes were envisaged, although, as noted above (Willets, 2010) these were not to be in place immediately and were only consolidated in the 2017 Higher Education and Research Act:

> *We will remove the regulatory barriers that are preventing a level playing field for higher education providers of all types, including further education colleges and other alternative providers. This will further improve student choice by supporting a more diverse sector, with more opportunities for part-time or accelerated courses, sandwich courses, distance learning and higher-level vocational study. It will also lead to higher education institutions concentrating on high-quality teaching, and staff earning promotion for teaching ability rather than research alone (DBIS, 2011, Executive Summary, para 9).*

While not mentioned specifically in the 2011 document, this reference to an equivalence of esteem for teaching staff (via a TEF), along with the encouragement of teaching-only institutions, was to form a major plank of the fifth stage of market reforms from 2016:

> *We will make it easier for new providers to enter the sector. We will simplify the regime for obtaining and renewing degree-awarding powers so that it is proportionate in all cases. We will review the use of the title 'university' so there are no artificial barriers against smaller institutions. It used to be possible to set up a new teaching institution teaching to an external degree. Similarly, it was possible to set exams for a degree without teaching for it as well. We will once more decouple degree-awarding powers from teaching in order to facilitate*

externally-assessed degrees by trusted awarding bodies (DBIS, 2011, Executive Summary, para 10).

We will put in place a new regulatory system that protects standards and quality, gives power to students to trigger quality reviews where there are grounds for concern, yet cuts back the burden of review for high performing institutions. The new funding environment also provides an opportunity to introduce a simple, transparent regime for all types of provider with the Higher Education Funding Council for England (HEFCE) taking on a new role as consumer champion for students and promoter of a competitive system. We will strip back excessive regulation on providers wherever it is possible including: reducing burdens from information collection; exploring whether it is possible to reduce the costs associated with corporation tax returns; and adopting a risk-based approach to quality assurance (DBIS, 2011, Executive Summary, para 14).

Once again, however, the system of SNCs had limited success in creating a market-like effect on applicant behaviour. The system was first refined (the quality margin was increased to ABB+ and above, further reducing the core allocations for those that recruited heavily from among high achievers) and then abandoned after two years to be replaced by a removal of the numbers cap from academic year 2015–16 (HM Treasury, 2013). Partly this was because of the delay in regulatory reform, which reduced the level of downward pressure on fees. It was also partly due to the underlying assumptions of the market among policymakers which perhaps underestimated the strength of the whole sector when focusing on the behaviour of just those institutions at the top of the distribution, and those perfidious consumers who failed to respond to market levers.

2.7. THE STRANGE DEATH OF STUDENT NUMBER CONTROLS

A Higher Education Academy report (Taylor & McCaig, 2014) into the impact of SNC and the wider marketisation of the sector and based on interviews with key institutional policymakers concluded that:

> *The introduction of the most recent student number control policy had not led to the anticipated market differentiation in fees or a general redistribution of higher achieving students (those with ABB or above) within the sector according to our respondents. This realisation no doubt influenced the decision to abolish SNC from 2015—16 and fund an additional 30,000 places in 2014—15 in the December 2013 Autumn Statement (HM Treasury, 2013), something not anticipated by research participants in the months beforehand, the majority of whom hoped for a period of stability (Taylor & McCaig, 2014, p. 18).*

Analysis shifted from an investigation of the early impacts of a governmental experiment in market-making to a policy post-mortem. The report sought to answer two questions: why did the market mechanism fail, and why did government lose patience with their experiment of increasing flexibility?

> *The answer, in part, may be that demand for higher education places still exceeded supply, with acceptances up to a record level: 495,600 full-time*

> *undergraduates in the UCAS 2013−14 admissions cycle (from 677,400 applications) exceeding the previous high of 492,030 in 2011−12 [...] Any downward market effect on prices was unlikely in these conditions. Average tuition fees for 2013−14 were £8,507 (£8,263 after fee waivers), virtually unchanged from their 2012−13 levels (Taylor & McCaig, 2014, p. 18).*

Even at the higher-achieving end, demand remained high in those post-1992 institutions which might have been expected to reduce fees. This was because many of the equivalent-to-ABB qualifications are BTECs, rarely considered for access to many of the more prestigious institutions, but more often accepted by institutions such as modern (but mid-ranking) post-1992 institutions that were expected to 'yield up' high achievers to the more selective elite. The HEA report noted that:

> *Overall in the first two years of the new financial regime and the operation of SNC, there had been little reported redistribution in student numbers from one part of the sector to another, with AAB and ABB redistribution largely taking place between pre-1992 institutions. HEFCE analysis from 2011 on the distribution of AAB+ students by mission group found that a redistribution of AAB+ places would be unlikely to make any impact beyond the selective pre-1992s institutions (Russell Group and 1994 Group universities) because most applicants with AAB+ grades already attended these institutions. Of 22 HEIs that enrolled over 50% of student AAB+ profiles in 2011, 17 were members of the Russell Group or 1994 Group and the other*

> *five were specialist colleges of higher education covering the arts, dance and music (Taylor & McCaig, 2014, p. 19; HEFCE, 2011).*

Demographic factors also worked against the success of the SNC regime: applicants with A levels were in decline, along with the numbers of 18-year-old school-leavers in the population (Matthews, 2013; Morgan, 2013), and UCAS data had revealed evidence of a higher proportion of lower-qualified students (i.e. BBB or below) being accepted at selective pre-1992 universities than in previous years (UCAS, 2013). More damningly for government assumptions, the research found that despite high 'sticker price' entry requirements declared by the most selective institutions (which help them achieve high league table rankings), the situation at admissions was somewhat more nuanced, and that a focus only on the highest entry grades, by shrinking the core, actually reduced the attractiveness of many disciplines:

> *The research presented in this report illustrates the extent to which arts, humanities and social sciences (the subject disciplines least likely to require ABB or above even at the most selective institutions) can be threatened by a concentration only on a margin consisting of 'high achievers' (Taylor & McCaig, 2014, p. 19).*

This was because the most highly qualified applicants were often in just a few subject areas, for example the STEM subjects. Any growth in those numbers would be at the expense of other subjects in a fixed allocation; all else, including institutions' statutory duty to provide places for EU students, and aspects of their individual 'mission' such as offering a full range of disciplines or WP, had to be accommodated within a shrinking 'core' allocation.

As one senior planner at a selective pre-1992 institution noted:

> *We have some areas of the university which are in subjects which, again historically, have not recruited as strongly as others. It's harder to get good computer scientists or sociologists than it is to get lawyers and economists [...] At the moment the university takes a very strong view that we're a broad-based university [...] at the moment there's no discussion around the possible closure of any particular subject area (Taylor & McCaig, 2014, p. 25) (emphasis added by author).*

This SNC regime can perhaps best be seen as:

> *[...] a policy intervention which focused on just a few variables: the number of students with ABB+ profiles attending selective institutions; the tuition fee charged by institutions to stimulate marketisation; and consumer choice in the system as measured by pre-existing instruments such as the NSS and the Destination of Leavers in Higher Education (DLHE) (Taylor & McCaig, 2014, p. 19).*

What of the effect of other aspects of the *Students at the Heart of the System* White Paper? Enhanced information for applicants was supposedly the key driver of choice, in the form of Key Information Sets (not actually launched until the second year of the new fees regime in 2013–2014). These largely worked as a collation of information already available: the Destination of Leavers from HE survey (DLHE) has been in use since 2002–2003 and the National Student Survey (NSS) since 2005. Institutions have long been responding to this information, to the extent that student satisfaction had already risen from 80% to 87% on average across the sector during the first decade of NSS (HEFCE, 2013).

2.8. SUMMARY

The third and fourth stages of marketisation significantly changed the discourses and likely impacts of differentiation by introducing a mechanism for price differential (variable fees and bursaries) and better indices of quality to enhance applicant choice in the form of surveys of student satisfaction (NSS) and graduate outcomes (DLHE) packaged in digestible formats for ease of comparison. Later, following the increase of fees in 2010 and the shift of policy responsibility from DfES to DBIS, the discourses of supply and demand, of return on investment and market segmentation (all of which implied that institutions should jettison poorly recruiting or low-tariff programmes) became more noticeable in policy statements. Once institutions had set their 2012–2013 fee levels in March 2011, market mechanisms to address them exhibited an air of desperation in the face of huge public finance liabilities due to rates of non-repayment being higher than expected (the Resource Accounting Budget). These mechanisms were in the form of short-lived 'High Grades' and 'Core-Margin' SNC regimes which met their 'strange death' within two years (McCaig & Taylor, 2015; McGettigan, 2013). Once again, as after the introduction of variable fees in the 2004 HE Act, a true market resulting in a reshuffling of applicants (demand) and places (supply) had failed to emerge, and in November 2013 the Treasury announced a removal of number caps and the advent of a demand-led open market (Table 2.1 and Table 2.2).

Table 2.1. Stage Analysis Table 'Diversity to Differentiation'.

Stage 3: From Diversity to Differentiation	Arguments Employed/Developed					
	Tuition Fees	Opening up the Market	Widening Participation	Return on Investment	Diversity	Measurable outcomes (Choice Signals)
2003 White Paper/2004 HE Act	Variable tuition fees introduced (deferred repayment scheme when earning £15,000) Students 'should contribute more' New income to drive expansion	£3k fees to stimulate market differentiation HEIs to 'play to strengths' Applicant choice drives market; consumer rights to information Reforms to make it easier to attain DAP and UT	OFFA Proportion of fee income to be spent on access Institutions to set own bursary levels (above min. £300)	English HE returns 'best in OECD' Students 'should contribute more' to costs of HE as primary beneficiaries	Celebrates move from elite to mass participation Expansion encouraged – but not just 'more of the same'	A national student satisfaction survey proposed (became NSS)

| 2009 White Paper DBIS now the parent Dept. | In wake of 2008 economic crash sets up a review of HE finance under Lord Browne | Number caps introduced. Growth for HEIs now dependent on choice information for applicants. Key role for Regional Development Agencies | Choice-driven information: knowledge of variable financial returns essential UNISTATs service improved. | HEIs encouraged to have diverse missions, teaching or research focus New Foundation degrees to help WP | HEIs should remove inefficient low number programmes STEM courses encouraged | NSS and DLHE as measures of performance/ aid applicant choice |

Table 2.2. Stage Analysis Table 'Competitive Differentiation'.

Stage 4: From Diversity to Differentiation	Tuition Fees	Arguments Employed/Developed				
		Opening up the Market	Widening Participation	Return on Investment	Diversity	Measurable Outcomes (Choice Signals)
Browne Review of HE finance (2010)	Remove the fee cap 'Soft-cap' of £12K Affordable at average fee of £7.5k	Remove the fee cap to stimulate real market effect	Sliding scale of income spent on access and success for highest fees (for those above soft-cap) Abolish OFFA — let HEIs decide WP priorities and spending levels	Market to decide	Need to differentiate HEIs — no specific mention of diversity	Market to decide

2011 White Paper	Fees set at £9k cap (the full cost of degrees now transferred to graduates) Deferred repayment scheme when earning £21,000 – more 'progressive' than previous regime	Need to reduce average fees to £7.5k by creating a free distribution Number controls to encourage shift of 'brightest' to 'best' HEIs Numbers allocated to those charging below £7.5k More choice – Key Information Sets, better UCAS course information	Mandatory bursaries abolished – don't aid recruitment Mandatory bursaries abolished National Scholarship Programme (fee waivers rather than bursaries)	More choice enables applicants to judge where to achieve best ROI	New 'alternative providers' encouraged to market	NSS and DLHE as measures of performance/aid applicant choice Encouragement of measures of teaching excellence

Table 2.2. (Continued)

Treasury announcement 2013	Abolition of the number controls Initial 60,000 extra places (as Browne had recommended); demand-led system from 2015–16

CHAPTER 3

THE HIGHER EDUCATION AND RESEARCH ACT 2017: THE ROAD TO RISK AND EXIT

3.1. INTRODUCTION

The fifth stage of market reforms embodied by the HERA represents a policy step change in three main ways, all of them derived from the opening up of the market from 2015–16 (HM Treasury, 2013) and the White Papers (2003, 2011) discussed in the previous chapters. First, it introduced the risk of institutional failure (and thus market exit) to the newly competitive marketplace. This came in several forms: risk for institutions was presented as a natural corollary of competition, including from institutions that had a greater reputation for teaching than for their research (the cornerstone of most league table rankings) and concomitantly more risk of failure. Risk was also clearly discursively shifted from the state (which had previously underwritten failing institutions) to the institutions and students. This in turn necessitated consumer protection for students, further adding to the costs of such failing institutions. However, risk was not to be borne equally: better performing institutions (including most existing universities and specialist HEIs), as measured by enhanced performance data monitoring, would be under reduced scrutiny, while those performing poorly would receive the kind opprobrium familiar to schools in receipt of poor OFSTED ratings. These risk indicators were expected to force institutions to reduce tuition fees or fear losing market share to new 'challenger providers'.

Second, HERA introduced a single regulatory regime for all HE providers (HEPs) including those previously referred to as HEIs, further education colleges and new 'alternative' or 'challenger' providers. This involved the abolition of existing funding councils (HEFCE and HEFCW for Wales) and regulators (OFFA for access and participation and the quality regulator QAA) with all these functions merged into the Office for Students (OfS) from 1 April 2018. Thirdly, HERA promoted the importance of teaching excellence as an indicator or signal for applicants where 'excellent teaching' could be found in the system. It became a condition of provider registration with the OfS that all HEPs engage in the TEF exercise from 2019–20. However, early plans to attach fee caps to the various TEF ratings (with the highest fee cap reserved only for Gold-rated institutions) were abandoned during the legislative process, and a subject-level TEF was piloted from 2017–18. This would eventually provide course-level applicant information but further dilute the original intention that applicants could easily differentiate HEPs by a single marker of teaching excellence. Taken together, these new mechanisms of competitive risk and the fear of market exit were designed to create a tuition fee differentiation to match the UCAS tariff differentiation, with only the 'best' providers justifying the highest fees and a long taper of other less-successful HEPs offering HE at lower price points.

3.2. RISK FOR APPLICANTS AND STUDENTS

Risk was presented not only as a stimulus for institutions; the Green and White Papers (DBIS, 2015, 2016a) made clear the risk that students would be taking on if they made the wrong choices, which in turn could harm the public finances. HE was now portrayed in such a way as to question whether it could be the automatic, life-changing route into remunerative professions of popular belief long-encouraged by governments:

> *Now that we are asking young people to meet more of the costs of their degrees once they are earning, we in turn must do more than ever to ensure they can make well-informed choices, and that the time and money they invest in higher education is well spent. [...]*
>
> *Recent indications that the graduate earnings gap is in decline, and that significant numbers of graduates are going into non-graduate jobs, reinforce the need for action. Higher education should deliver lasting value to graduates — and to the taxpayers underwriting the student loan system (DBIS, 2015, Foreword by Minister of State for Universities and Science, Jo Johnson MP).*

Spelling out these implications for potential applicants marks a radical departure from previous policy statements and suggests a degree of ambivalence about further widening participation (WP). Equally, this is an important signal to those without the highest entry tariff points either to enter alternative routes (i.e. apprenticeships) or opt for less costly HE provision:

> *Demand continues to be strong for employees with high level skills; over half of the 14.4 million jobs*

> *expected to become vacant between 2012 and 2022 are in occupations more likely to employ graduates. However, at least 20% of graduates are not working in high skilled employment three and a half years after graduation (DBIS, 2015, Executive Summary, para 6).*

Once again, the provision of more accurate and relevant information to applicants and students is the key to choice; however, the discourse of the Green Paper made it clear that this choice should be between attending and not attending HE:

> *We recognise that higher education is not the only option for young people, so it is essential that they have the best information and support available to be able to make these huge decisions (DBIS, 2015, Executive Summary, para 11).*

This would be reinforced by the principles for reforming the HE architecture which most clearly made the case for state intervention in the HE system:

> *The government intervenes in higher education because of: i) information asymmetries between students and institutions and insufficient demand side pressures to ensure quality; ii) the inability of students, in the quantities desirable for society and the economy, to finance higher education at the point of entry without support; and, iii) the broader benefits to society of having a highly educated population (DBIS, 2015, Part C; para 6).*

This combination of stressing the importance of less costly HE (for both the consumer and the government) and the importance of informed choice about alternatives is enhanced by an exhortation that the system should offer applicants a guide to 'information regarding the quality of teaching they are likely to experience and what this is likely to mean for their future employment' (DBIS, 2015, Part C; para 11), which introduces a major theme of the Green Paper, *The Teaching Excellence Framework*:

> *Currently, not all universities assign teaching the same significance that they give research. Significant funding is allocated through the Research Excellence Framework (REF) to universities who deliver high quality research. There is no mechanism in place to reward teaching, resulting in a lack of focus on providing a high quality student experience. Some rebalancing of the pull between teaching and research is undoubtedly required: this should not be at the expense of research, but through additional incentives to drive up teaching quality (DBIS, 2015, Part C; para 20).*

> *The new Teaching Excellence Framework (TEF) aims to recognise and reward high quality teaching. [...] The TEF will increase students' understanding of what they are getting for their money and improve the value they derive from their investment, protecting the interest of the taxpayer who supports the system through provision of student loans. It should also provide better signalling for employers as to which providers they can trust to produce highly skilled graduates (DBIS, 2015, Part C; para 21).*

The purpose of the *Teaching Excellence Framework*, as laid out in the opening section of the Green Paper, was to provide a measure of teaching quality in order to financially reward those that scored well on TEF assessments and also to drive failure and exit for those that did not. It would 'identify and incentivise the highest quality teaching to drive up standards in higher education, deliver better quality for students and employers and better value for taxpayers' (DBIS, 2015, Chapter 1, para 1.3). As with the 'core and margin' SNC regime introduced in *Students at the Heart of the System* (discussed in the previous chapter), competitive expansion would accrue to some institutions, while those that failed would suffer financially and be replaced by new providers that were necessarily more likely to raise quality:

> *The TEF should change providers' behaviour. Those providers that do well within the TEF will attract more student applications and will be able to raise fees in line with inflation. The additional income can be reinvested in the quality of teaching and allow providers to expand so that they can teach more students. We hope providers receiving a lower TEF assessment will choose to raise their teaching standards in order to maintain student numbers. Eventually, we anticipate some lower quality providers withdrawing from the sector, leaving space for new entrants, and raising quality overall (DBIS, 2015, Chapter 1, para 1.4).*

As well as improving the overall quality of teaching in the system, the reward of teaching-only (and thus cheaper) providers would help to widen access as it would also:

> *recognise those institutions that do the most to welcome students from a range of disadvantaged backgrounds, support them to remain on their courses (such students are often at a higher risk of dropping out) and help them to progress to further study or a high skilled job (DBIS, 2015, Chapter 1, para 1.3).*

Even as the Green Paper celebrated the potential gains from introducing risk to the existing hierarchy of institutions through the application of quality, it was hoped that the TEF would not only drive further price differentials but also 'fix' the WP problem of higher levels of dropout among those poorer and under-represented social groups. Thus, WP students are relegated to an issue of concern only to less prestigious institutions because, as the designers of the 2011 White Paper similarly believed, those least likely to benefit in professional career terms from HE should only be aiming for lower cost provision. However, as noted in Chapter 2 of this volume, HEA research into the impact of the number controls regime actually found that the distribution of those with higher grades (AAB and above) did not actually match the distribution of incomes and thus the archetypical 'WP student':

> *Often the distribution of ABBs was skewed heavily towards some disciplines (sciences, Subjects Allied to Medicine) that recruit quite strongly from WP backgrounds, while other disciplines popular with those from non-WP backgrounds (arts and humanities, social sciences for example) are less likely to recruit those with ABB or above (Taylor & McCaig, 2014, para 4.1, p. 23).*

While that earlier, short-lived scheme did acknowledge that the move from AAB to ABB brought even more WP students into the favoured 'high grades' margin, it did so at the expense of subject breadth. In short, the SNC regime did not make much difference to the distribution of WP students (on average more likely to have sub-ABB grades), but it did threaten the existence of entire disciplines at prestigious pre-1992s that had very buoyant demand from more advantaged young people. This scenario emerged in a demand-led system based on the notion that choice is sovereign. Nor did the 2011 regime recognise how important WP was to institutional missions. One Head of WP at a pre-1992 Russell Group university noted that: 'academic schools shouldn't waste lower offers if they didn't need to' (Taylor & McCaig, 2014, 24).

Such institutional policy actually benefited WP students precisely because many of them were in fact applying to study on high-tariff courses at the expense of courses attracting a lower tariff popular with more financially and socially advantaged young people. Highly ranked institutions were happy to maintain and celebrate WP and thus didn't much baulk at the centralisation of admissions policy, but they did baulk at the notion of squeezing out entire disciplines as the 'core' of those below ABB shrank in the second year of number controls; in some pre-1992 institutions, over 60% of applicants presented with ABB or above. Institutional disquiet at the impact of the regime — probably through the backstairs lobbying of the Russell Group — is most likely the reason that the system was scrapped so quickly, to be replaced by an uncapped, fully demand-led system from 2015 (HM Treasury, 2013).

3.3. RISK FOR INSTITUTIONS: REGULATORY REFORM

Risk becomes the key element in associating WP with bad outcomes for the individual applicants who, as we have seen, are reminded that they would benefit least from HE, but also for the institution because WP students are expensive to teach and are more likely to drop out, and for the economy because if more WP students attended cheaper provision the average tuition fee would fall. Risk really comes into its own in those elements of the consultative Green Paper: Part B *Opening the Sector to New Providers*, which outlined the need for a single route into HE for all HEPs. Within the single route, HEPs could choose between three models of regulatory relationship with the new OfS, specifically over quality assurance and ability to set fees. This was further developed in the White Paper in the form of three kinds of provider status (DBIS, 2016a, Box 1.1):

Registered 'Basic' status will be available to providers who want to be officially recognised as HE providers but do not want to access government funding or student support, or obtain a Tier 4 licence. Their courses must match the academic standards as they are described in the Framework for Higher Education Qualifications (FHEQ) at Level 4 or higher, and they must subscribe to the independent student complaints body, the Office of the Independent Adjudicator (OIA). This will provide a degree of consumer confidence in these providers that is not present in the current system. Providers wishing to access public funding for their courses and/or students, or wishing to be able to make an application to the Home Office for a Tier 4 licence, or have degree awarding powers (DAPs) or university title (UT), will first need to be approved. They will be able to choose between two models, based on what best fits their operation:

Approved provider status will allow an institution's students to access up to £6,000 tuition fee loans per year or, if the institution does well in TEF, the inflation-adjusted annual cap. Approved providers will be able to set their fees at any level. Becoming an approved provider will require: successful quality assurance (QA) through the Quality Assurance Agency (QAA) until 2017–2018 and through the new QA framework from 2018 to 2019; financial sustainability, management and governance (FSMG) checks; meeting the Competition and Markets

Authority's requirements regarding students' rights as consumers; and adherence to the OIA's good practice framework.

Approved (fee cap) provider status will cap an institution's fees. There will continue to be a basic cap of up to £6,000 per year and a higher cap of up to £9,000. In each case, if the institution does well in TEF, the inflation-adjusted annual cap would apply. As is currently the case, these providers will be required to agree an Access and Participation Agreement with the OfS if they want to charge fees above the basic cap. Eligible students at these institutions will be able to access loans to cover all of their fees. These providers will be eligible to receive grant funding from the government, including the research funding for English providers currently offered by HEFCE, which will in future be allocated by UK Research and Innovation. In addition to the requirements for approved status, approved (fee cap) providers will need to comply with more stringent FSMG requirements, comparable to those currently required of HEFCE-funded providers in line with the HE Code of Governance. If they receive government grant funding, they must also be able to demonstrate their compliance with the relevant terms and conditions of that funding, so that OfS can give assurance to Parliament of appropriate use of public funds.

However, the Basic category was subsequently dropped as too (financially) risky for new 'challenger' providers, with no alternative measures proposed. According to analysis by the Higher Education Policy Institute, this would in fact leave more providers unregulated (602) than regulated (531) (DBIS, 2016b; OfS, 2018; WonkHE, 2018).

This policy shift during the legislative process between the passing of the Act and the development of regulatory frameworks (DBIS, 2016b) failed to fully satisfy the requirement for a single framework containing all the market levers within the purview of a single regulator (the OfS) for all HE in the system. While a large number of providers would remain outwith the official register, they would nevertheless be able to compete with existing providers by meeting the new (lower) requirements to attain DAPs and UT. These could be achieved far more quickly and with lower proportions of HE students than under previous regulations, even for those new providers not on the OFS register. Risk, in this case, was to take the form of ongoing OfS checks of enhanced monitoring data. In each case, it would be up to the provider to take the risk that they could meet, and continue to meet, certain conditions:

> *A provider with a limited evidence base, but which met 'model 2' expectations around quality, student protection, information provision and financial stability, might still be able to secure DAPs, but potentially on a rolling, time limited basis, with regular monitoring. They may have some restrictions placed on them, for example not being able to validate degrees at other providers, continued restrictions on visa conditions for international students, or being restricted to certain subjects.*
>
> *Another provider with a more substantive evidence base, and which met the 'model 2' expectations, might secure DAPs on a 6 yearly renewable basis, with only light touch monitoring, and few or no restrictions (DBIS, 2016b, para 13).*

As with the rest of HEPs in the established sector, the balance of regulatory oversight would reduce with successful performance as an incentive for such providers to take on the risk of expansion (something that was not universally welcomed by alternative providers and was reflected in the government's own impact assessment – DBIS, 2016b). In cases of failure, DAP rights could be withdrawn:

> *Conversely, an incumbent provider with DAPs, whose performance gave cause for concern, could be put into a period of more extensive monitoring, with this signalled clearly to all relevant parties. Where DAPs are renewable, the time period could be shortened; or DAPs could be removed from any provider, in the most serious cases (DBIS, 2016b, para 2.13).*

Stimulating greater use of DAPs in the immediate term, government wished to 'do more to remove barriers to securing DAPs in the near term'. This included:

> *[...] reviewing the current four year track record requirement with a view to reducing it to three years. We will also consider introducing more flexibility on what constitutes track record, for example taking account of models other than the traditional validation route (DBIS, 2016b, para 2.14).*

Meanwhile the Green Paper proposed that those providers able to satisfy the conditions for DAP be more easily enabled to adopt UT, at a lower tariff:

> *The current student numbers criterion for university title specifies that, in order to be eligible, an applicant should have 1,000 full time equivalent*

> *higher education students of which at least 750 are studying for a degree and 55% of the organisation's overall student body is studying higher education (DBIS, 2016b, para 2.18).*

Again in an echo of the 2011 White Paper, which promised 'year-on-year' further liberalisation of student numbers, the Green Paper held out the prospect of eventually abolishing number conditions for UT:

> *We want to introduce access to university title for a wider range of providers and take the view that universities should not be so limited by the size or location of the student body. For this reason we propose reducing the number of students or potentially even removing the student numbers criterion for university title (DBIS, 2016b, para 19).*

Enabling easier access to DAP and UT for new providers was clearly designed to drive the supply side of the market; both would make it easier to develop new programmes of study in response to demand. The use of UT would give such providers a competitive edge over other HE providers, for example specialist HEIs that have never used UT or further education colleges that also offered HE programmes.

3.4. CAVEAT EMPTOR: THE BUYER TAKES ON THE RISK

While entry to the status of HEP could represent a risk for institutions if they proved unable to satisfy quality assurance requirements to maintain that status, institutional exit from the system carried obvious risks both for students and for the state. A system driven even more by applicant choice would likely create the conditions under which a provider may need to exit the system 'perhaps as a necessity or alternatively through its own choice. "Exit" may happen at provider, course or campus level' (DBIS, 2016b, para 2.2). This was discursively presented as a natural corollary of market conditions:

> *In a changing and more competitive sector, providers that innovate and present a more compelling value proposition to students will be able to increase their share of total students — in some cases this may be at the expense of other institutions (DBIS, 2016b, para 2.3).*

'Compelling value' is the proposition most likely to appeal to those with lowest entry grades, those who, as noted above, would read the TEF signals of where less remunerative HE experiences were to be had, and 'buy' accordingly. The crude sorting mechanism of the 2011 White Paper is here replaced by something much starker based on the assumptions that cheaper providers were in turn the ones most liable to fail. *Caveat emptor* (literally 'let the buyer beware') transfers the risk that a product or service may fail to meet expectations on to the applicant consumer.

The return on investment calculation for applicants was to be made easier by the use of Longitudinal Education Outcomes (LEO) data, derived from HM Revenue and Customs data on the tax returns of those that enter any post-16 educational programmes. The Small Business, Enterprise and Employment Act (2015) enabled the DfE in 2017 to publish raw data presenting graduate earnings by characteristics such as sex, ethnicity, age, home region and prior attainment at A level and, more radically, by subject choice and institution (McGettigan, 2018). Andrew McGettigan notes that:

> *LEO's first cohorts left university in 2003/04 and it is now possible to look at their earnings 1,3,5 and 10 years after graduation. The figures for subsequent cohorts covered such years as they were able, with 2008/09 graduates the most recent with 5-year figures.*
>
> *[in June 2017] LEO data was updated to show earnings breakdowns for course and institution combined. That is, it became possible to look at the earnings of Social Studies graduates from the University of Sunderland compared to those who had studied English at Durham, but only up to five years out of university (McGettigan, 2018, online).*

LEO data therefore adds significantly to the corpus of market signalling and thus to the ability of applicant consumers to make informed choice; where to find 'compelling value' and where to 'beware'. Where consumers fear to tread, of course, HEPs may be obliged to exit the market.

The discourses of *Fulfilling our Potential: Teaching Excellence, Social Mobility and Student Choice* sought to portray 'exit' not as market failure but evidence of a better functioning market system: 'removing provision may indeed lead to it being replaced by higher quality provision' (DBIS, 2015, para 2.4). However, the abstract language of failure and exit as the corollary of low quality ignores the lived reality of 'students from a range of disadvantaged backgrounds' who, as noted above (DBIS, 2015, Chapter 1, para 1.3), are most likely to attend 'lower quality' institutions which in turn 'support them to remain on their courses (such students are often at a higher risk of dropping out) and help them to progress to further study or a high skilled job' (DBIS, 2015, Chapter 1, para 1.3). Clearly it is applicants and students from 'disadvantaged backgrounds' that are invited to choose on price to attend HEPs that will not only bear the greatest burden (in terms of supporting those most likely to drop out) but which are thus the most likely to 'fail' to remain competitive in such a marketplace. The alternative to taking on the biggest burden of risk is, for such students, not to attend HE at all.

Naturally, such a system had to come with consumer protection but with the important precondition that 'in designing student protection, we would seek to ensure that the regime does not create unnecessary barriers to exit' (DBIS, 2015, Chapter 1, para 2.6). Public expenditure was as important here as protection for students:

> *The outcomes Government will want to see are that students and the reputation of the sector are protected as well as minimising any impact on public finances. This student protection should primarily be focused on academic continuity (i.e. ensuring the student can go on to continue their study), but failing that could be financial (i.e. recompense which protects the student from complete financial loss, which may include tuition fees, maintenance etc.) (DBIS, 2015, Chapter 1, para 2.7).*

The proposal is to introduce a 'requirement for providers to have contingency arrangements in place, which set out what their approach and commitments would be to the student in the event of a provider exit, or course or campus closure' (DBIS, 2015, Chapter 1, para 2.8). The contingency arrangements would be expected to apply in any type of course closure or exit and should cover the following:

> *Continuity of provision for the student – offer the student an alternative course or support them in*

> *organising an alternative course at another provider — which the student accepts. It would be up to each institution to define how it would achieve this, for example, collaborative or bilateral agreements with other institutions or awarding body (DBIS, 2015, Chapter 1, para 2.8).*

This proviso — that institutions should enter partnerships with competing institutions, in effect guaranteeing that they would absorb courses and students from each other in the event of competitive failure — potentially implied a system of 'credit accumulation and transfer', long ago envisaged by the Higher Education Quality Commission (HEQC, 1995) in a precompetitive era (see Chapter 2). Logically incoherent, not to say intellectually incompatible with the prevailing discourses of competitive differentiation, this proviso showed the limitations of market thinking in two ways.

Firstly, as the proviso was envisaged as a requirement only for a subgrouping of the newly unified HEP sector (nowhere was it suggested that, for example, Oxford and Cambridge need enter into such an agreement), it introduced quite different regulatory requirements for only some providers, when in theory any HEP could be competitively undercut by alternative, cheaper providers. Incidentally, this was contradicted by 'Simplifying the higher education architecture: The principles for reform' summary, which stated that 'under this new regulatory framework, there would no longer be different regulations for different types of providers' (DBIS, 2015, Chapter 1, para 4.22) although, as noted above, this principle did not hold in all respects.

Secondly, a guarantee of continuing provision of a course at a given HEP flew in the face of institutions' autonomy about what to offer and how they choose to provide it, again entrenched in the principals for reform of the architecture, one of which was to 'create an open, market-based and affordable system, with more competition and innovation' (DBIS, 2015, Chapter 1, para 4). The system thus envisages two sectors: one which is autonomous, innovative and competitive on quality; and one which is heavily regulated to meet state outcomes in relation to costs and the needs of the labour market – in effect, a return to the binary divide.

Consumer protection and recompense, however, is essential to the functioning of markets, and once again it is not the state taking on the risk:

> *If a student does not accept a new place, then the provider must give the student a rebate for the (unspent prepaid tuition fees) with recompense being made in the same way it was paid (direct to student if directly paid or to SLC if it was a loan). This could be achieved by the provider in a number of ways, for example: an insurance policy, a bond, reserve funds, or Escrow accounts (DBIS, 2015, Chapter 1, para 5).*

This could not be drawn in too onerous a manner, of course: 'Any such requirement would need to be carefully designed so as not to create a barrier to new entrants' (DBIS, 2015, Chapter 1, para 2.8). Thus, the system had to allow for easy access and exit, yet not place actual existential risk to the graduate experience of individuals (however much it may be disrupted by the transfer system) nor threaten the public finances.

3.5. DEVELOPING DISCOURSES: FROM THE GREEN TO WHITE PAPER AND ACT

Following a four-month period of consultation over the Green Paper, the White Paper *Success as a Knowledge*

Economy: Teaching Excellence, Social Mobility and Student Choice (DBIS, 2016a) appeared in May 2016. The White Paper was 20 pages shorter than its predecessor, having dispensed with the technical language of the consultative Green Paper: having decided on the content for the White Paper, government set out to present arguments in support of its positions and focused mainly on aspects of reform that required legislation in preparation of the Bill put before Parliament in the first months of 2017. The HERA came into effect in June 2017.

This section considers structural changes in the use of arguments put forward to justify the policy shift. The most striking change between Green and White Papers was the relative position of arguments relating to the TEF, which formed the opening section of the 2015 document (from p. 18) but only appeared as part of the second section of the 2016 document (first appearing on p. 40). While the TEF caused by far the most disquiet within the sector, not least because of the technical difficulty of producing a measure of teaching excellence and the threat that it would represent to academic autonomy, it now appeared after a lengthy exposition of measures that a competitive HE market would emerge in which the TEF had only a small part to play.

Several new arguments and phrases were employed in the White Paper. As well as a return of emphasis on diversity (this time of institutions and provision), the document made use of a triumvirate of phrases evoking the notion of 'producer capture': incumbency; inflexibility; and anti-competitiveness. Each of these was portrayed as behaviours common to existing providers that formed barriers to the fullest exposition of the competitive market:

> *Competition between providers in any market incentivises them to raise their game, offering*

> *consumers a greater choice of more innovative and better quality products and services at lower cost. Higher education is no exception.*
>
> *There is no compelling reason for incumbents to be protected from high quality competition. We want a globally competitive market that supports diversity, where anyone who demonstrates they have the potential to offer excellent teaching and clears our high quality bar can compete on a level playing field. If we place too much emphasis on whether a provider has a long established track record, this by definition will favour incumbents, and risks shutting out high quality and credible new institutions (DBIS, 2016a, Executive Summary, paras 7–8).*

Collusion was similarly evoked as an example of producer capture, here in the use of an academic critique of the American HE system:

> *There is a risk, as highlighted by David Palfreyman and Ted Tapper, that the combination of financial and cultural factors in the HE teaching system result in our higher education provision becoming less demanding. They cite the example of the 'crafty mutually convenient disengagement contract among distracted academics and instrumentalist students' that has emerged in part in the American higher education system. We must act pre-emptively to ensure that this risk of disengagement, which undoubtedly already exists in part, is not allowed to take hold systemically (DBIS, 2016a, Executive Summary, para 24).*

In the absence of internal systemic drivers of higher quality indicated above, the English system would be driven by applicant choice to ensure quality. The role of the state was to let the converse of the choice-quality couplet — competitive failure — happen where necessary. This was to be crucial to the way that institutions could differentiate themselves in the marketplace:

> *Information, particularly on price and quality, is critical if the higher education market is to perform properly. Without it, providers cannot fully and accurately advertise their offerings, and students cannot make informed decisions. But there is currently little pressure on providers to differentiate themselves in this way. This is a cause for concern as poor decisions by the student as to which course and institution to attend can prove costly not just for them but for the broader economy and the taxpayer (DBIS, 2016a, Executive Summary, para 19).*

> *The possibility of exit is a natural part of a healthy, competitive, well-functioning market and the Government will not, as a matter of policy, seek to prevent this from happening. The Government should not be in the business of rescuing failing institutions — decisions about restructuring, sustainability, and possible closure are for those institutions' leaders and governing bodies (DBIS, 2016a, Executive Summary, para 17).*

The White Paper also continued to develop a harder-edged rationale for the centrality of student choice, largely focused around students' future employment prospects. Once again applying market rationalism to a group that had seemed ambivalent about utility maximisation at the time of the

2011 reforms (DBIS, 2011; Taylor & McCaig, 2014), the White Paper chose to focus on graduate premia outcomes:

> *For competition in the HE sector to deliver the best possible outcomes, students must be able to make informed choices. Universities provide an environment for deeper and wider learning, allowing for the development of analytical and creative thinking, objective inquiry and primary research. But evidence suggests that for most students, the most important outcome of higher education is finding employment. The teaching students receive can transform their life chances, as demonstrated by the strong graduate premium, and low graduate unemployment rates (DBIS, 2016a, Executive Summary, para 18).*

As with the Green Paper, which first drew attention to the possibility that some consumers would benefit from alternative routes into employment, variable graduate outcomes were highlighted, citing new research that suggested that 'while the graduate premium is still significant and was sustained over the recession' there was evidence of 'huge variance in graduate earnings depending on choice of subject and institution, as well as background'. This was enough, according to the White Paper, to suggest that 'some graduates are not in jobs most suitable to their skills' (DBIS, 2016a, Executive Summary, para 19).

The reference to variation by student background could be taken to acknowledge the well-evidenced role of social background characteristics in determining all manner of life chances, but where earlier policy statements evoked such an observation to suggest the HE system could do more to ameliorate inequalities of outcome (e.g. NCIHE, 1997;

DFES, 2003; HEFCE, 1994, 2000; HM Government, 2004), in this context it could be interpreted as a subliminal link between disadvantaged backgrounds and certain kinds of post-16 educational journeys. Certain routes were not only a waste of time and money for the student, but also a case of the 'taxpayer underwriting the student loan system' as Jo Johnson pointed out in the Foreword to the Green Paper.

3.6. A RISK-BASED QUALITY SYSTEM

Central to the 'robust risk-based system' of quality control was the careful measuring of monitoring data required of all registered providers:

> *Building on the light-touch annual monitoring currently carried out by HEFCE — in future to assess a range of indicators that give assurances and raise red flags about shifts in provider activity or behaviour, or failure to meet a range of input and output benchmarks. be done by the OfS — all providers will be subject to annual data monitoring by the OfS to assess a range of indicators that give assurances and raise red flags about shifts in provider activity or behaviour, or failure to meet a range of input and output benchmarks (DBIS, 2016a, Box 1.5).*

Indicators were to include: graduate employment; progression to professional jobs and postgraduate study; student retention levels; student completion levels; student recruitment levels; degree outcomes; student entry requirements/UCAS tariff data; National Student Survey results; number of complaints to the OIA; and TEF scores. In effect this monitoring of outcomes would eventually produce a more sophisticated set of institutional league tables by which applicant consumers could select the most appropriate programme of study and HEP.

These data (now including LEO returns data from the tax system, as noted above) would actuate one of the key aims of the Green and White Papers to create an evidence base that demonstrates the value of individual HE programmes, creating the apogee of applicant information:

> *For the first time we will link higher education and tax data together to chart the transition of graduates from higher education into the workplace better. This rich new data source will give students the information about the rewards that could be available at the end of their learning, alongside the costs. This innovation is at the heart of delivering our reform agenda ambitions: improving choice, competition and outcomes for students, the taxpayer and the economy (DBIS, 2016a, para 34).*

Following the passage of the HERA (HMSO, 2017), the OfS came into being in April 2018 (under Sir Michael Barber) and began issuing the regulatory framework necessary to make the market work:

> *It is not our role to guarantee the future success of the higher education sector and no amount of central direction could do so. Two vital ingredients are critical to the health of our higher education sector — institutional autonomy and academic freedom — and the OfS will protect and promote both (Sir Michael Barber, Foreword, OfS, 2018, p. 10).*

While Barber's introductory remarks focused on autonomy and freedom rather than engaging in directly marketised discourses, the Framework document returned to familiar themes by linking autonomy, dynamism and innovation to student choice:

> *The OfS's approach to regulation puts informed student choice and institutional autonomy at its heart. It sees the dynamic of providers responding to informed student choice as the best mechanism for driving quality and improvement, and will regulate at the sector level to enable this. The OfS will regulate at provider level to ensure a baseline of protection for all students and the taxpayer. Beyond that threshold the OfS will encourage and enable autonomy, diversity and innovation (Sir Michael Barber, Foreword, OfS, 2018, p. 16).*

The centrality of the regulatory function was underlined by the inclusion of consumers in the operation of the Framework: student representatives are not only invited to contribute to the design of market mechanisms (such as the TEF) but also to oversee (perhaps as internal 'watchdog') efforts to improve access for the disadvantaged:

> *At sector level, the OfS will create conditions for informed choice, competition and improvement in several ways, including: involving students in the way it regulates; working with a designated data body to help students make the best choices; operating the Teaching Excellence and Student Outcomes Framework (TEF) to incentivise the improvement of the quality of teaching; and removing unnecessary barriers, including regulatory ones, to entry for high quality new providers. It will*

also regulate to create space for innovation, use a range of indicators to evaluate the health of the sector and use its teaching grant funding strategically, for example to improve access for students from the most disadvantaged or underrepresented backgrounds (Sir Michael Barber, Foreword, OfS, 2018, p. 17).

3.7. SUMMARY

The fifth stage of marketisation introduces the discourses of 'risk' and 'exit' to make the differentiated market fully competitive; however, it also goes beyond the use of discursive argumentation to exhort marketised behaviours among providers and consumers. The shift from a system lightly regulated by a funding council acting at arms length from government to a system in which both funding and regulatory control (including of quality assurance) exist within a single body – the OfS – can be seen as an act of centralisation that threatens its declared *raison d'etre* of fostering institutional autonomy and academic freedom. However, the potential of the Act can only really be discerned in relation to its secondary purpose of creating a differentiated distribution of HEPs demarcated by tuition fee level. Hence, the risk-based regulatory system reduces the burden on those providers that are already successful but punishes providers that cannot demand higher tariff entry; only this latter group are obliged to reduce their fees, cut provision or go into administration. Only this latter group are threatened with replacement by new, cheaper providers ushered in by the legislation. Exit and replacement are the only motive mechanisms to reduce tuition fees, and the negative effects on students without the necessary UCAS tariff points are merely the price government demands to retain untrammelled autonomy for those providers at the upper end of the distribution (who, thus protected, will feel no need to innovate). The fifth stage thus appears as a final 'throw of the die', piling more responsibility onto applicants, making it easier for new providers to offer a 'University' titled education, producing more pressure for existing providers to reduce the breadth of their subject offerings. Pace Barber, however, the operation of this market requires more, not less, central direction than ever before (Table 3.1).

Table 3.1. Stage Analysis Table 'Risk and Exit'.

Stage 5: Regulating for Choice and Quality, Differentiation Driven by Risk	Arguments Employed/Developed						
	Risk	Choice	HE participation	Quality in Teaching	Human Capital	Efficiency and Accountability	Regulatory Regime
DBIS (2015) DBIS (2016) HM Government (2017)	Risk-based regulation allows for less oversight of best-performing HEPs, more oversight of poor-performing HEPs Exit allowed for failing institutions – a positive market outcome New challenger HEPs encouraged – DAP	More information about economic returns for each course LEO Narrower range of courses as HEPs concentrate only on what is viable	WP students best served by low-cost providers HE not for everyone – some courses offer low Return on investment so should consider if lowly rated HE is worth it Increased range of providers adds to diversity of system	TEF to help rebalance teaching and research and make HE more responsive to consumers' needs Producer capture; incumbency a threat to competitiveness	Opening up of the market expands the numbers	Two-year degrees encouraged – into labour market with less debt Driven by risk incentives – poorest courses would close. Price competition from new providers should drive down overall costs and thus public spending outlay (affordability at average fee of £7.5k across system) Inflexible practices (rewarding research rather than teaching)	OfS merged from HEFCE and OFFA but with only a regulatory function Maintain register of all HEPs and collect monitoring data based on performance

and UT easier to achieve

TEF to drive behaviour – poor performers could lose students

Poorly performing HEPs could go to wall "leaving space for new entrants, raising standards overall"

TEF ratings to enable applicant choice

New challenger HEPs offer more choice at different price points

Poorest performers allowed to fail; could lose DAP and UT

CHAPTER 4

CONTINUITY AND DISCONTINUITY ON THE ROAD TO RISK AND EXIT: STAGES OF MARKETISATION IN COMPARATIVE POLICY ANALYSIS

The preceding chapters of this book have outlined the varying arguments used by governments to justify or rationalise the application of market mechanisms in the English HE system, and particularly the market for undergraduate students. This final chapter sets out a critical policy discourse analysis that addresses the following set of questions: to what extent has there been a continuity of policy from the encouragement of efficiencies and accountability in the 1980s to the emphasis on competition and risk in 2017? Was there an intention among policymakers that the system would have to go through incremental stages of marketisation to reach the 2017 position? Was it designedly cumulative; i.e. as part of a deliberate and phased policy of neoliberalisation of the sector? Alternatively, has marketisation developed in response to factors beyond the control of policymakers, with government essentially reactive? What role has the introduction of tuition fees paid by students (and subsequent increases) played in the development of marketisation? What, if anything, does the English case tell us about the nature of neoliberalism or indeed the future trajectories of other national systems in the process of marketising and differentiating their institutions?

In exploring these questions, the book has identified five distinct stages of marketisation. Although they can be seen as chronologically following on from each other, they cannot be seen as part of a planned, linear process. That would imply that each stage was a necessary prerequisite for the following stage and would then disappear having achieved its aim. Instead, the preceding analysis has shown that in many cases the underlying assumptions of each stage remain, albeit subsumed to greater or lesser extent as the next wave of market reforms takes centre stage. In this sense, the various stages form building blocks that underpin the current edifice, as can be seen from the preceding narrative. However, this book is primarily concerned with why the English system has been marketised in the way that it has been; why governments employed this or that methodology, designed this or that funding incentive or policy lever at that particular time. The answer to that meta-question challenges any notion of a 'grand design' deliberately operationalised by successive governments, not least because many of the market reforms were clearly responding to external factors and the arguments deployed in governmental discourses were post hoc rationales rather than rational or even ideological actions.

4.1. ANALYSIS: THE FIVE STAGES OF MARKETISATION

The following section employs political discourse analysis to explore the underlying discourses used to justify marketisation and reveals the arguments that have been variously employed at different times, and sometimes for different purposes, over the time period.

Stage 1 (1986–1992)

Stage 1 can be seen as the efficiency and accountability stage of marketisation. This stage began with the application of private sector business-style practices encouraged within the public sector. The wider discursive rationales employed centred on the national need to optimise human capital in the face of globalised competition. The final act of this stage of marketisation was the 1992 Further and Higher Education Act, designed to divest the state of direct responsibility for HE and encourage diversity of provision and providers. New public management discourses were introduced to HE policy via the government-commissioned Jarratt and Croham reports (1986 and 1987) which acted across several dimensions, as follows.

Key Discursive Elements
Centralisation versus autonomy: The Jarratt and then Croham reports recommended that the University Grants Committee (UGC) be replaced with a University Funding Council (UFC), thus ensuring that business influences would be represented in the public management of the university sector, acting as a check on autonomy. They also recommended an end to academic tenure, threatening the permanence of individual academics' contracts and allowing

universities to close academic departments, freeing them up to develop a wider range of provision in their place. This would enable:

Efficiency in public services as the new UFC could henceforth steer universities and polytechnics to develop new programmes that responded to public demand, but also to meet government's own requirements for highly skilled human capital and ensure Britain's national competitiveness. The system was undergoing a period of returning growth after a decade of retrenchment, and while this was encouraged in policy it would necessarily have to occur within strict cost controls. In order to drive efficiencies and make provision more relevant to the needs of the economy, funding would no longer be in the form of the traditional 'block grants' (which gave institutions autonomy about what they did with the funding). Instead, Jarratt and Croham signalled the need to shift to a funding model in which providers would have to competitively bid to provide services on behalf of the state.

New sources of income would also have to be sought by institutions, partly to offset lower units of resource (per-student funding) envisaged as the system expanded, but also to offset potentially lost provision. Accelerating a trend identified in the United States as 'academic capitalism', this tendency for institutions to diversify business income sources into other services such as offering professional degrees, applied research, knowledge exchange activity and the greater exploitation of estates (e.g. for conferences and other public events) also encouraged individual academics to become more entrepreneurial by offering their services as consultants.

The 1987 Education Reform Bill and 1988 Education Reform Act (ERA, 1988) furthered these agendas by creating a Polytechnic Founding Council (to match the UFC) with business representation on the board and consolidated the shift from block grants to a service provision model of funding. Foregrounding the continuing reduction in unit costs, the Act encouraged universities and polytechnics to develop as regional power bases, serving the national human capital requirements for a high-skills economy.

The final element of the first stage was the 1992 Further and Higher Education Act which reformed the policy landscape in several ways. In relation to the centralisation versus autonomy debates that were the focus of the 1980s reviews and the Education Reform Act (1988), the decision to end the binary divide between universities and (public) polytechnics on one level offered greater autonomy to the latter (along with FE colleges, they were previously under direct state control) and, like the universities, they were encouraged to be more innovative and market-responsive in their offer of provision. Former polytechnics could also now, for the first time, award their own degrees. While HEIs in the new enlarged sector were encouraged and steered towards taking a leading role regionally and even nationally, both sides of the former binary divide were now invited to compete for student numbers. It is important to recall that this new policy landscape was designed specifically to diversify higher education as well as to drive efficiencies and accountability, while the existing peer-review system was assumed to continue to guarantee quality across the unified system.

Summary

Over the six-year period between 1986 and 1992 (a period in which the percentage of 18 to 21-year-olds in the system grew from 15% to 33%, McCaig, 2000), market interventions in the name of efficiency and accountability and to better encourage human capital growth already exhibited a sense of contingency and even contradiction. Presumably a pro-marketisation state could have engineered the shift away from a rigid binary divide, with one side under government control, to the competitive marketplace of the post-1992 era without all the intervening policy upheaval. As Walford (1988) noted in Chapter 1, perhaps the greater central control of all the levers of the binary system was a necessary precondition for the ensuing liberalisation, although it appeared to contemporaries as an incoherent enmeshing of the ideological preference for privatisation (New Public Management) and the political need to concentrate all powers (and suppress all opposition) in the name of greater national competitiveness.

Stage 2 (1992–2000)

Stage 2 can be described as the 'celebration of diversity' period of marketisation. Discourses in this stage were drawn from HEFCE statements throughout the decade and also the Dearing Review which reported on the cusp of the change from a Conservative to Labour government in 1997.

Key Discursive Elements

Centralisation versus autonomy continued to be a key theme as the newly unified system evolved and expanded. HEFCE statements from inception (e.g. HEFCE, 1994) were enthusiastic and encouraging of diversity initially, albeit with caveats introduced later in the 1990s that the state could not always afford to support diversity 'for its own sake'. In 1997 the Dearing Review proposed extending the regulatory role of the state, in the form of a Quality Assurance Agency (QAA) and a Credit Accumulation and Transfer system that would allow students to move smoothly between degree programmes and institutions. This represented a severe curtailment of institutional autonomy, particularly for those pre-1992 established universities that were the locus of arguments, suggesting that 'more means worse' in the newly expanded sector. As early as 1994, two 'mission groups' were established to represent the discrete interests of research-intensive universities, foreshadowing the moves towards greater differentiation in the following decades.

Efficiency and accountability for public spending also remained to the fore; however, the introduction of partial tuition fees in 1998 was expected to release more income for institutions and Labour's decision to abolish maintenance grants at the same time was designed to reduce the public burden of a growing sector. Meanwhile institutions were exhorted to develop and offer alternative sub-degree provision and by the end of the 1990s the state made it clear that student numbers would be controlled, with allocations dependent on previous performance (e.g. HEFCE, 2000), which in effect put a cap on the amount of diversity encouraged.

Diversity was discursively encouraged and largely celebrated as a 'good thing', although often as a means to other policy ends. WP became a central policy aim of the whole HE sector in the late 1990s. This was argued for in several ways, for example in the name of social justice (post Dearing and the Labour government) or in the form of innovative curricula designed to meet the needs of the economy and to provide new modes of learning for HE applicants from nontraditional backgrounds. In policy terms, WP was discursively supported by – and supportive of – the global movement to encourage 'lifelong learning', encapsulating the human capital notion that all modern economies would require their labour forces to periodically retrain in order to remain competitive. Diversity was also encouraged in overtly marketised discourse, as a means by which institutions could create niche provision and thus add to the breadth and social utility of the sector, but it would only be encouraged when it could be justified by demand and when it could be delivered cost-efficiently.

Quality, long absent from policy discourses, featured for the first time in the debates around the Dearing Review

(1996–1997), particularly in its considerations of the future size and shape of the HE sector. Representations from the Russell Group of selective, research-focused institutions and the old universities staff trade union (the Association of University Teachers) used submissions to Dearing to raise questions about how quality could be assured across such a diverse sector. Along with the freedom to charge higher fees, quality (expressed as the need to maintain the excellent global reputation of British higher education) became central to the later differentiation stages of market reforms. Labour in government adopted the Dearing suggestion of a QAA which would ensure that standards were judged in the same way across the sector (arguing against autonomy) but did not take up more radical proposals to allow credit accumulation and transfer, which required acceptance of equal quality across the sector.

Summary

This stage embraced the consolidation of a diverse system which offered expansion and promised to meet national human capital requirements. However, by the end of the period the necessity of reforming the funding of the sector brought forth arguments around quality and centralised control, as an interventionist Dearing Review and Labour government sought to use the system to shape society in relation to both social justice and national competitiveness. Representatives of the old 'pre-1992' part of the sector actively sought differentiation, manifested in their arguments over quality and top-up tuition fees.

Stage 3 (2000–2010)

Stage 3 covers the period that discursively shifted from diversity to differentiation and the introduction of a market. This stage represents a major step change in policy and its underlying discourses and arguments. As noted in Chapter 2 of this volume, the introduction of partial fees paid by students (£1,000 per annum, representing about 25% of tuition costs) took place against a backdrop of some established research universities threatening to charge top-up fees. Given that the Labour government exempted many students from low-income households from paying these fees, institutions received less fee income than had been expected. Therefore, the lobbying for much higher 'variable fees' proceeded even before the basic fee was introduced and the concept embedded. Higher variable fees were justified in the 2003 White Paper with arguments asserting that the principle that students should contribute to their own HE had already been established and could now be built on in the name of fairness. Several new (and some old) key discourses were used to actuate an HE market, as follows.

Key Discursive Elements

Opening up the market was central to the arguments employed to justify variable fees as a key signal of market differentiation; applicants would see the variable tuition price (between £1,000 and £3,000) and know where the 'best' higher education was to be obtained. Those institutions able to justify the higher fee were expected to be those that played to their strengths, in terms of excellence as measured in international comparative league tables. Variable fees would empower applicants to make better choices based on the provision of better consumer information to be hosted on UNISTATS, a government website. Plans to make it easier for alternative providers to attain their own Degree Awarding Powers (DAPs) and eventually University Title (UT) were also first raised in the 2003 document, further differentiating the range of HE options by providing competition for some of the poorest-performing 'new' post-1992 universities.

Another key market mechanism, allied to applicant choices, would be a set of measurable outcomes against which HEIs and even individual departments and courses could be judged. The 2003 White Paper introduced the idea of a national student satisfaction survey (NSS) as a measure of quality, and this was augmented by a Destination of HE leavers survey (DLHE) allowing applicants to see which degree programmes (from which institutions) were most likely to lead to remunerative careers. Relative positionality in terms of these market signals helped institutions to differentiate their offer, aided by the first appearance of domestic institutional league tables from 2005.

WP remained central to the discourse, given that the rise in tuition fees was expected to deter applicants from the poorest backgrounds. Government addressed this in two ways. On the one hand, it provided additional funding for collaborative partnership outreach work to encourage more applicants from groups under-represented in HE (the national Aimhigher programme, which many saw as creeping centralisation and a threat to institutional autonomy). The second major policy initiative – the creation of an Office for Fair Access (OFFA) – was only introduced in response to Labour backbenchers' criticisms of reform plans. However, once OFFA was established and given the role of regulating access expenditure including financial support (bursaries) for the poorest, government decided that there should be a market in bursaries, with each institution invited to set its own level (above a mandatory minimum), thus differentiating approaches to access and outreach.

Efficiency and accountability discourses were still present in these arguments: in a positive sense, the variable fee system was justified by a reiteration of the greater 'return on investment' available to English students as a 'graduate premium', said to be the highest in the OECD. Given the ever-increasing costs associated with a system that would only expand under these market incentives, buoyant returns for students justified higher fees as they were the primary beneficiaries of this expansion.

Diversity was still celebrated as the mechanism by which the English system had transformed from an elite to mass system, and market logic demanded that HEIs should be encouraged to differentiate by developing their own missions, for example whether to focus on teaching or research. Diversity was not to be encouraged if it just produced 'more of the same'. One aspect of diversity was the provision of vocational, labour-market-focused HE and the new (sub-degree) foundation degree (launched in 2001–2002) and this was expected to be taken up by FE colleges (often in partnership with existing HEIs) to help the system attain the 50% HE 'young participation' target by 2010.

The policy rhetoric of market differentiation continued in the 2009 White Paper *Higher Ambitions*; however, following the economic crash in 2008, the public expenditure context changed. Student number controls were introduced and government announced a review of HE funding and student finance, under Lord Browne (to report after the following election).

Under the new overall capped system, it was made clear to institutions that key information for applicants was even more important to any institution wanting to grow numbers; ever more choice information was to be provided via an enhanced UNISTATS service which was to include knowledge of the financial returns on investment for every course. The discourses around the concept of diversity necessarily hardened, with HEIs now invited to remove provision where courses did not attract viable numbers. Centralisation was evoked in a partial recognition that the market may not always best provide optimum levels of human capital;

government reiterated its support for Regional Development Agencies and invited HEIs to work more closely with them, and science, technology, engineering and mathematics (STEM) subjects were actively encouraged.

Summary

The 'diversity to differentiation' stage clearly represented a break from the benign management of a relatively well-functioning and well-regarded HE system. Dearing, the incoming Labour government (with its social justice agenda) and the impact of tuition fees each implied greater state intervention in the system; however, the prevailing mechanisms introduced in the two White Papers (2003 and 2009) and 2004 HE Act each fostered the imposition of market thinking. This extended to creating (against much opposition) a market in bursaries, based on the notion that the difference between a £300 and £400 bursary was going to make a difference to where applicants chose to study given the dozens of other variables. The alternative, a national bursary scheme offering the same level of support to any student from a low-income household, was simply not a 'market' solution and was thus discounted. The need to use market mechanisms to differentiate between HEIs was dominant among policy-makers in 2003, yet it had not been prominent in policy statements prior to the 2003 White Paper (see for example HEFCE's 5-year plan, HEFCE, 2000). It seems likely that established pre-1992 universities (represented by the Russell Group and the 1994 Group) and their allies in the sector — who had long lobbied for variable or top-up fees prior to Dearing as we have seen in Chapter 2 — were the driving force behind differentiation post-unification, and that a Labour government, keen not to antagonise key policy actors at a time when it needed selective institutions to embrace the national imperative to widen participation, went along with differentiation through market-like incentives as the only way to square the circle.

Stage 4 (2010–2015)

Stage 4 became the age of competitive differentiation within the emerging market. This stage can be seen as a continuation of Stage 3, but was based on two new recognitions. Firstly, the competitive elements of the market introduced in Stage 3 had palpably failed to create visible market signals of differentiation such that applicants were persuaded to shift their application decision-making, nor indeed had persuaded institutions to set fees variably, as policymakers had assumed. Secondly, the impact of the economic crash after 2008 had transformed the public spending landscape to such an extent that the system would either have to seriously contract or graduates would have to take on even more of the financial burden. Once again, marketised discourses designed to introduce more competition in the system framed the only viable solutions, but as with Stage 3 the underpinning arguments and rationales for reform were essentially reactive to external events rather than representing a rational progression from the past to a better future.

Key Discursive Elements

Tuition fees were the most contested and difficult issue that governments had to deal with after 2010 when the basic fee rose from £1,000 to £6,000 and the variable fee cap from £3,000 to £9,000. The Browne Review (2010) had recommended something much closer to a competitive open market in fees in order to stimulate a price differential that would create a parallel between tuition costs to the graduate and UCAS tariff points on entry, referred to by McCaig in Bowl et al. (2018) as a 'dual-price mechanism'. In the event, given the economic crash and subsequent public expenditure regime of austerity, the Conservative and Liberal Democrat Coalition Government (elected in May 2010) settled on a £9,000 maximum variable fee and introduced a more 'progressive' repayment regime for graduates. One thing that did survive from Browne was the calculation that even if average fees settled around £7,500 (the affordability level), around 40% of graduates would never pay back all their loans, simply because they would not earn above the new higher thresholds for long enough before loans were written off. The need to reduce average tuition fees to something close to the £7,500 figure has been central to all policymaking since 2011.

Opening up the market further was rationalised by Browne in two ways. First, removing the upper fee limit would allow a fee distribution to open up, based on the economic principle that the existence of a cap naturally encourages institutions to set prices as close to the cap as they can without losing market share. Second, by creating new funded places to expand supply to meet demand, competition would be generated from below. However, the government baulked at expanding student numbers in a period of austerity and by retaining a cap was confronted with institutions setting fees close to the maximum (£8,365 in the first year of the new regime). The 2011 White Paper was therefore an exercise in designing a set of student number controls (SNCs) that attempted to incentivise the best-qualified applicants (with higher UCAS tariff points) to attend only the best-performing institutions, and simultaneously incentivised poorer-performing institutions to lower their fees by offering additional student numbers at below the key figure of £7,500. The main competitive mechanisms were once again to be information and guidance for applicants, this time augmented by Key Information Sets and more relevant information on UCAS application course pages.

WP was again exhorted as an aim, although stripped of its earlier links to the benefits of social diversity. Taking its cue from Browne, the government chose to abolish mandatory bursaries in order to free up institutions from state direction about how they should widen participation or ensure 'fair access' (access not denied on the basis of social characteristics such as age, gender, sex, sexuality, religious belief, disability, etc.) State-funded WP programmes such as Aimhigher and Lifelong Learning Networks were discontinued in 2010 and 2011, partly rationalised by public spending cuts. This development, long lobbied for by the Russell Group and others, also made it easier for selective universities to focus their access spending on their own differential needs – in other words, to act competitively rather than collaboratively. Access spending was still regulated by the OFFA (Browne had wanted the regulator abolished) but henceforth there would be less emphasis on financial support and outreach, and more focus on supporting students in the system (retention) and helping them into postgraduate employment (discursively described as success in new policy rhetoric) (OFFA, 2011). In order to help reduce average fees, OFFA bursaries were to be replaced by 'fee waivers' which did nothing to support students from low-income households but did marginally reduce the level of repayable student loans they would face as graduates.

Return on investment – representing the transposition of the notion of efficiency and accountability onto the individual fee-paying student – remained discursively present in the form of a still-buoyant graduate premium. However, applicants were exhorted to use all the available sources of research into the variation in remuneration from different institutions and courses to make sure they did not encourage poorly performing institutions to charge more than they should. Consumers were expected to use their market power to 'shop around' for best value if they were unlikely to attain the higher grades.

Diversity in this stage is used only in the context of the encouragement of new 'alternative providers' who would come to the market to bid for the 20,000 places earmarked for institutions offering provision at below £7,500 or the open-ended numbers of courses made available for those wishing to offer HE at below £6,000.

Summary

As with the key market reforms of Stage 2, the various incentives based on SNCs and the opening up of new cheaper alternatives failed to create a competitive market effect. Very few highly qualified applicants changed their intentions or destinations as a result of the 'high grades' SNC policy, nor did prestigious universities elect to refocus their broad provision only on subject disciplines that attracted the very highest grades. Some refused to engage in what was in effect a zero-sum game of swapping numbers on one course for numbers on another, preferring to consolidate existing numbers rather than abandon subject breadth. Consequently, very few 'middle-ranking' institutions lost highly qualified students to 'higher-ranking' institutions and thus felt no market pressure to go 'down-market'. The Department of Business, Innovation and Skills had to quickly retrench on the costs of unregulated cheap sub-degree provision encouraged by the White Paper (McGettigan, 2013) and efforts to encourage alternative providers were stymied by the lack of legislation that would create a level regulatory playing field for all providers (the subject of Stage 5). The failure to create a functioning market in undergraduate places despite several major policy initiatives and the consistent application of marketised discourses over a 15-year period reached its apogee in November 2013 when the Treasury unexpectedly announced the discontinuation of number controls; instead it provided funding for an immediate 60,000 additional places in the next academic year and a fully open, demand-led market from academic year 2015–16. While there were clear discursive and intellectual continuities with the previous stage, and a sense that Stage 3 incentives would inject a more competitive form of differentiation than Stage 2, the effects of the crash and the subsequent need to deal with higher than anticipated fees under the new variable cap rendered Stage 4 of marketisation an incoherent failure even on its own terms.

Stage 5 (2015–)

Stage 5 introduced competitive differentiation driven by risk and exit. This stage features a larger degree of actual legislative and regulatory change than Stages 3 and 4 and in some ways can be seen as the culmination of the policy reforms introduced as long ago as the 2003 White Paper. The HM Government (2017) introduced a level playing field for a wide range of registered providers and thus fully opens the sector up to competition. Theoretically, this competitive environment can either lead to the replacement of poorly performing providers with new 'challengers' or add to the overall capacity in the system, to the extent that supply meets latent unmet demand or even creates new demand. Either outcome is assumed to be sufficient to reduce average tuition fees in the system by applying price competition at the lower-performing end of the distribution; however, as with the successive hikes in the variable fee cap in 2004 and 2010 and number control incentives after 2011, the 2017 Act contains no mechanism to persuade the large bulk of existing HEPs to reduce tuition fees. The following summary of Stage 5 will focus on the major policy arguments used to rationalise reform and highlights both new and reappearing sets of discourses.

Key Discursive Elements

Risk and Exit are the two major innovations introduced in this latest stage of marketisation policy. Risk refers to the operation of regulatory oversight that HE providers (HEPs) will be subject to. The application of risk is differentiated by HEPs' performance against a set of outcomes data, largely pre-existing but expanded to include Longitudinal Economic Outcome (LEO) data that use tax records to assess the likely return on investment an applicant can expect. Those HEPs that perform well in monitoring will represent less risk and face less regular QAA checks; those that perform poorly will be subject to more oversight and interventions from the Office for Students (OfS). Interventions will include an order that poorly performing HEPs enter into credit transfer agreements with neighbouring HEPs similarly benchmarked on performance. This would ensure that, in the event of course closure or the financial failure of the HEP, students are able to complete their programmes of study at a similar provider; alternatively, they will be financially reimbursed for the undelivered portion of the programme.

The main form of competition is expected to come from new HEPs that can henceforth attain their own DAP and UT more easily. Failing providers would be allowed to exit the market (whereas previously they would have been propped up by the funding council) 'leaving space for new entrants, raising standards overall' (Chapter 3 above) in the discourse of the 2016 White Paper, neatly combining the previously unconnected notions of price (the new provider is assumed to be cheaper) and quality. Other forms of competitive pressure are featured in the 2017 Act. The Teaching Excellence Framework (TEF), which grades providers as Gold, Silver or Bronze, is expected to impact HEP behaviour by ensuring teaching and learning have equivalent status to research. Much was made in the discourse around the TEF in the initial

2015 Green Paper about the possibilities of changing conceptions of what makes a 'good university', although in practice TEF rankings (which did in fact show that many post-1992 providers performed better than traditional pre-1992 universities) can be appealed and the introduction of subject-level TEF ratings is likely to obscure any simple message about the quality of a given institution.

Choice for applicants is once again the main discursive element that will drive competition and eventually determine the level of risk and possibility of exit. As noted above, there will be more and better information for consumers (LEO, TEF subject-level ratings) but in this iteration the discourse of choice is evoked in the now wider range of providers operating at different price points and offering alternative provision such as two-year degrees. However, the expansion in the choice of providers could meet its counterpoint in a narrowing range of provision as existing providers are encouraged to jettison financially unviable courses and many new providers come to market offering only a restricted choice of subjects (Evans, 2015, 2016).

WP is also evoked problematically in relation to choice; in the discourse of the 2016 White Paper, new providers at advantageous price points may be the best option for WP students who traditionally present with lower entry qualifications and are often from low-income backgrounds. More affordable HE is thus presented as a solution for those that present with lower UCAS tariff points. More positively, the newly increased number and range of providers adds to system diversity and any increase in the number of students satisfies the demands for greater human capital.

Return on investment is another key choice consideration. For the first time the Green Paper (2015) and following White Paper (2016) introduce the notion that HE may not be for everyone, and that applicants with low entry qualifications should think carefully about the return on investment of some degree programmes from poorly performing providers. Other options are available for such applicants, thanks to the new suite of choice information. This marks a major discursive shift from the 2011 White Paper which extolled the financial benefits of higher education for the individual, something routinely expressed as a 'graduate premium' in every policy statement since Dearing and the introduction of fees in 1998.

Quality in teaching has a more central role in the discourse of marketisation than was the case in earlier documents. In addition to the TEF (which drives consumer choice), the White Paper evokes the notion of producer capture in the form of collusion between academics, students and institutional managers that can threaten competitiveness in a system by protecting incumbent providers.

Efficiency and accountability are assured by many provisions of the new regime, and these discourses are employed in relation to both students and HEPs. Two-year degrees will enable students to enter (or re-enter) the labour market more quickly and with less debt. HEPs will benefit from the closure of poorly performing courses and can instead invest in provision with higher demand and more remunerative outcomes for all. Price competition from cheaper new providers, it is assumed, will reduce the average tuition fee, perhaps to the level of affordability assumed by government of £7,500 per annum, thus reducing the public subsidy used in writing off graduate debts.

Summary

This fifth stage of marketisation can be seen as the necessary regulatory framing to actuate reforms going back as far as the 2003 White Paper, yet the radicalism of the latest stage only highlights the failure of those earlier market reforms to significantly shift applicant and institutional behaviours. Many thousands of highly qualified applicants still choose to apply to and attend what policymakers would consider 'suboptimal' HE destinations for well-rehearsed socioeconomic and cultural reasons (Bowl et al., 2018). Also, many of the system's most prestigious universities choose to adhere to pluralist notions of what a university is for, rather than streamlining their provision to focus only on degree programmes that require the very highest UCAS tariffs. Similarly, market assumptions ignore the highly regarded (and selective) provision offered by HEPs across the distribution, albeit in lower concentrations. Driven mainly by the economic imperative of reducing the average tuition fee, government prefers to open the floor below 'poorly performing' providers by introducing mechanisms of 'risk and exit', with better applicant information the only motive factor.

4.2. DISCUSSION: CONTINUITIES, DISCONTINUITIES AND REIMAGININGS IN MARKETISATION DISCOURSES

The preceding thematic policy discourse analysis of 12 policy documents over a 30-year period has produced nine distinct discursive themes. Analysis of these themes indicate some continuity of discourses while others have been discontinued and some are discursively 'reimagined' in relation to changed contexts. The following section looks at continuities, discontinuities and reimaginings that are represented as discourse shifts to rationalise policy reform.

4.2.1. Centralisation versus Autonomy

These dichotomous discourses have been ever-present across the five stages of marketisation (**Table 4.1**), although

Table 4.1. Centralisation versus Autonomy.

Discursive Themes	Stage	Discourse Shifts
Centralisation vs autonomy	1	1986–1988 – centralisation via business interests on boards.
		1992 – autonomy reimagined: polytechnics and FE colleges set free from state control (1992 F&HE Act).
	2	1997 – centralisation reimagined to rationalise Dearing and Labour's WP policies; student number controls.
	3	2003 – autonomy: market decides; 2009 – centralisation: number controls; autonomy: demand-led system.
	5	2016 White Paper/2017 HERA – OfS regulatory framework and monitoring.
		2018 – OfS increases regulation and monitoring of performance.

noticeably there have been periods when autonomy was stressed, as during the passing of the 1992 Further and Higher Education Act in 1992 (Stage 1) which transferred powers from the central state to the polytechnics, colleges of higher education and FE colleges, resulting in the transition of the former into universities. Later, in the run-up to the 2004 HE Act (Stage 3), autonomy was discursively used to further the introduction of a competitive, differentiated market as HEIs were encouraged to establish positions in the 'variable' fee market regime. At most other stages in the marketisation process (Stages 2, 4 and 5), the dominant policy outcomes have been to centralise powers in the state to meet national social and economic needs, even to centralise powers in order to create the regulated market that exists since 2017.

4.2.2. Efficiency in Public Services/Individual Return on Investment

Efficiency in public services was only a factor during the first two stages of reform when business interests were seen as important in invigorating the HE sector (the evocation of New Public Management thinking), but also have to be seen in the context of system expansion after years of retraction (Table 4.2). Once HEIs began to receive more income directly from students and were encouraged to differentiate in a competitive market, efficiency in public services became less relevant; here the discourse shifts into a concern that the student/consumer, as the key choice-maker, is reminded that she/he is the prime beneficiary and is provided with enough information to make the optimal decision.

4.2.3. Funding Mode

As with discussions about efficiency, the discourses of state funding changed fundamentally after the earliest stages with the introduction first of a 'service provision' model of university funding in place of block funding (Stage 1) and the onset of competition (Table 4.3). The shifting burden of the costs of HE from the state to the individual graduate (Stages 2–4) led to new discourses extolling the benefits of the 'graduate premium'. However, the state has continued to fund economically critical STEM subjects and activities designed to widen participation and, of course, also continued to underwrite student loan debt. Fees, then, are used discursively to help

Table 4.2. Efficiency in Public Services/Individual Return on Investment.

Discursive Themes	Stage	Discourse Shifts
Efficiency in public services	1	Business representation on UFC and Polytechnics' Funding Council boards. Growth expected to continue at lower unit cost.
Return on investment (for the state)	2	1998 – fees introduced: growth expected to continue, more fee income released for institutions. 2000 – control over student numbers; allocations based on previous performance.
Return on investment (for individuals)	3	2003 White Paper/2004 Act – English HE returns 'best in OECD'; students 'should contribute more' to costs of HE as primary beneficiaries. 2009 White Paper – choice-driven information: knowledge of variable financial returns essential. UNISTATs service improved.
	4	2011 White Paper – more choice enables applicants to judge where to achieve best return on investment.
	5	2016 White Paper/2017 HERA – two-year degrees encouraged – into labour market with less debt; more information about economic returns for each course LEO and TEF ratings. HE not for everyone – some courses offer low ROI so applicants should consider if low-rated HE is worth it.

Table 4.3. Funding Mode.

Discursive Themes	Stage	Discourse Shifts
Funding mode	1	1986 – block grant.
		1987 – reimagined: moves from block grant to service provision model.
		1988 and 1992 – service provision: state as customer, institutions as providers.
	2	1997 Dearing – fees to be paid by students at 25% of cost of degrees, keep maintenance grants.
		1998 Labour government – £1,000 fees (with exemptions for poorest) but remove grants.
		2000 – additional HEFCE funding for WP students to reflect cost of teaching.
	3	2004 – variable tuition fee cap £3,000 introduced (deferred repayment scheme when earning £15,000).
	4	2009 – Browne Review of fees suggests removing fee cap.
		2010 – Government applied new variable fee cap of £9,000 (deferred repayment scheme when earning £21,000).
	5	2016 White Paper/2017 HERA.
		2018–2019 – review of tuition fees.

create the fee differential thought necessary to actuate a real market distribution of providers, and at the same time necessitate even greater regulatory oversight in the form of student finance reviews such as the one begun in 2018 (Stage 5).

4.2.4. New Sources of Income

The discourses of privatisation, monetisation and academic capitalism were, like the New Public Management ideology that pervaded Stage 1, part of the reimagining of the HE sector as more dynamic and entrepreneurial in keeping with the political context (a third-term 1980s Conservative government) (**Table 4.4**). However, the state also encouraged HEIs to engage in new curricula development to satisfy national economic policy (Stages 2 and 3) and this exhortation extended into Stage 5 when two-year degrees,

Table 4.4. New Sources of Income.

Discursive Themes	Stage	Discourse Shifts
New sources of income	1	1986–1987 – academic capitalism encouraged – don't rely solely on state block grants.
		1988 – universities and polytechnics to develop as regional power bases.
		1992 – new universities (post-1992s) take on more regional labour market role – free to develop curriculum to meet local/regional demand.
	2	1997 Dearing – develop new vocational curricula in response to needs of labour market.
	3	2001 – new (sub-degree) foundation degrees launched.
	5	2017 HERA – two-year degrees encouraged – into labour market with less debt.

reimagined as a new source of income (although they had been encouraged and abandoned twice before in the 1990s and 2000s, due to the lack of student demand), were promoted in the context of offering value-for-money options for applicants.

4.2.5. Human Capital

The discourses around the development of human capital exhibit a similar trajectory to those around new sources of income (Table 4.5). While human capital development was clearly central to the rationale of a publicly funded system in place during Stages 1 and 2, the period of competitive differentiation and occasional student number caps placed most of the onus on individual HEIs and applicants; the market was supposed to determine the balance of highly skilled graduates during Stages 3 and 4. Interestingly, however, the discourse of expansion as a result of the opening up of the market, where supply would finally meet demand, was partly couched in terms of meeting national human capital needs.

Table 4.5. Human Capital.

Discursive Themes	Stage	Discourse Shifts
Human capital	1	1986 and 1987 – efficiency driven by need to grow the system.
		1988 ERA – need to focus on local and regional labour markets.
	2	1997 Dearing – Lifelong learning promoted as a good.
	5	2016 White Paper/2017 HERA – opening up of the market expands the numbers.

4.2.6. Widening Participation — Diversity as a Good

WP, a societal project that acknowledges and aims to correct historical inequalities in access to HE in Britain, is a realisation of the dual benefits of diversity: of both institutional types and of the student body. Diversity was a natural concomitant of the unification of the HE system in 1992 (Stage 1) and an equally natural outcome of expansion. Not only were a broad range of disparate institutions now encouraged to provide higher education, the increased participation rate implied wider participation which implied a more diverse student body. During Stage 2 these developments were both celebrated in policy discourses and encouraged by funding incentives (Table 4.6). However, during Stages 3 and 4, diversity 'for its own sake' largely

Table 4.6. Widening Participation: Diversity as a Good.

Discursive Themes	Stage	Discourse Shifts
WP/diversity as a good	1	1992 F&HE Act — diversity of student body encouraged.
	2	1994 HEFCE statement encouraging diversity.
		1997 Dearing and Labour government — WP encouraged.
		1999 — Government introduce requirements from HEIs to say what they are doing to widen participation and state-funded WP programmes.
		2000 — HEFCE statement that diversity must be justified by demand and efficiency 'not just more of the same'.

Table 4.6. (*Continued*)

Discursive Themes	Stage	Discourse Shifts
	3	2003 White Paper — HEIs encouraged to have diverse missions, teaching or research focus; celebrates the shift from elite to mass participation.
		2004 Act established OFFA to regulate access; proportion of fee income to be spent on access; institutions to set own bursary levels (above min £300).
		2009 White Paper — HEIs should remove inefficient low-numbers programmes; STEM courses encouraged.
	4	2010 Browne Review — HEIs need to differentiate provision and access work; let HEIs decide WP priorities and spending levels.
		2011 White Paper — mandatory bursaries abolished; National Scholarship Programme (fee waivers rather than bursaries).
		2011 White Paper — new 'alternative providers' encouraged to market.
	5	2016 White Paper/2017 HERA — opening up of the market expands the numbers; new challenger HEPs encouraged — DAP and UT easier to achieve; increased range of providers adds to diversity of system.
		2016 White Paper/2017 HERA — WP students best served by low-cost providers; HE not for everyone — some courses offer low ROI so should consider if low-rated HE is worth it.

disappeared from policy documents to be replaced by the imperative of market differentiation. Ironically, in Stages 4 and 5, the discourse of differentiation incorporated the need for new providers to come to market — in effect diversifying the sector in a different register. While system diversity was celebrated at the tail end of Stage 1 (the end of the binary divide) because it introduced private sector dynamism and reduced the burden on the state, in Stages 4 and 5 diversity is employed mainly as a mechanism of the much wider project of increasing low-cost supply.

4.2.7. Quality

The discourses around quality emerged only at the onset of the unification of the system in 1992 (Stage 1) and in Stage 2 were evoked mainly in relation to how the quality of the English system could be made compatible with such a wide range of institutions and with an expanding number and diversity of students that had not succeeded academically during their secondary schooling. This debate subsided over time to a certain extent, not least because by maintaining high entry requirements many of those most concerned about quality were able to avoid contact with those applicants with low UCAS tariff points (**Table 4.7**). Neither Dearing nor the incoming Labour government threatened institutional autonomy over admissions. As with the discourses of human capital and diversity, the use of quality in policy discourses shifts away from a concern for the overall sector during Stages 3–5, where quality (in the form of indicators of teaching excellence) is evoked mainly as an aspect of institutional market positionality. The 'risk-based' regulatory system also seeks to acknowledge and celebrate 'world-class higher

Table 4.7. Quality.

Discursive Themes	Stage	Discourse Shifts
Quality	1	1992 F&HE Act – rejects fears of diluted quality in newly expanded sector.
	2	1997 – Dearing and Labour government reject overtly market solutions on quality. Creates QAA to ensure quality is assured across the sector.
	3	2003 White Paper – a national student satisfaction survey proposed (became NSS).
		2004 Act – NSS and DLHE as measures of performance/aid applicant choice.
	4	2011 White Paper – encouragement of measures of teaching excellence.
	5	2016 White Paper/2017 HERA – TEF to help rebalance teaching and research and make HE more responsive to consumers' needs; producer capture; incumbency a threat to competitiveness.
		2018 – OfS to collect monitoring data based on performance; poorest performers allowed to exit market.

education' by reducing regulatory oversight for the best-performing providers.

4.2.8. Tuition Fees

While debates on tuition fees have often proved politically and economically toxic for governments, the discussions are treated quite instrumentally in policy discourses. During Stage 2, Dearing and the Labour government rationalised the need for fees on the dual basis that institutions needed more money and it would not be coming from the straitened public purse; students should be expected to contribute to the costs of HE given that they were the primary beneficiaries (Table 4.8). Very similar arguments were employed during Stage 3: indeed the 2003 White Paper merely noted that the 1998 introduction of fees had already established the principle; raising the fees and making them variable would only increase the return on investment for graduates. The shifting of the full cost burden of tuition onto graduates in 2010 required a different approach. It was partly justified by the political need to reduce public spend after the 2008 crash, of course, but discursively tuition fees are mainly used as a mechanism by which the system signals variations in quality, essential for the workings of any market.

Table 4.8. Tuition Fees.

Discursive Themes	Stage	Discourse Shifts
Tuition fees	2	1998 – tuition fees introduced at £1,000 (25% of cost); exemptions for poorest students.
	3	2004 Act – variable fees (up to £3,000) introduced; deferred graduate repayment scheme.
	4	2010 Browne Review/Government announcement – variable fees rise to £9,000 with 'more progressive' deferred graduate repayment scheme.

4.2.9. Opening Up the Market and Choice for Applicants

The HM Government (2017), Stage 5, clearly represents the culmination of policy reforms designed to open up a competitive differentiated market (Table 4.9). The principle of expanding the number of providers of HE and the need for better mechanisms of informed choice appeared in the

Table 4.9. Opening Up the Market and Choice for Applicants.

Discursive Themes	Stage	Discourse Shifts
Opening up the market/ choice for applicants	3	2003 White Paper and 2004 Act — £3k fees to stimulate market differentiation; HEIs to 'play to strengths'; applicant choice drives market; consumer rights to information. Reforms to make it easier to attain DAP and UT.
		2009 White Paper — number controls introduced; growth for HEIs now dependent on choice information for applicants.
Measurable outcomes and choice signals	4	2010 Browne Review — remove the fee cap to stimulate real market effect (not adopted).
		2011 White Paper — SNCs to stimulate differentiation and new providers encouraged to market; more choice — Key Information Sets, better UCAS course information.
		2013 Treasury — abolition of the number controls; 60,000 new places; open market from 2015 to 2016.

Table 4.9. (*Continued*)

Discursive Themes	Stage	Discourse Shifts
Risk and exit	5	2016 White Paper/2017 HERA – new challenger HEPs encouraged – DAP and UT easier to achieve; new challenger HEPs offer more choice at different price points; poorest performers allowed to fail; could lose DAP and UT. Narrower range of courses as HEPs concentrate only on what is viable; TEF ratings to enable applicant choice.

discourses of Stages 3 and 4, and the inclusion of TEF ratings and LEO metrics in Stage 5 are additive rather than real step changes. However, there have been changes in the wider economic context that required subtly different discourses; following the crash and the introduction of number controls in 2009 (Stages 3 and 4), responding to the market by expanding provision necessitated 'playing to strengths', which implied that institutions should make hard-nosed business decisions. Conversely, the removal of number caps from 2015 to 2016 meant that in Stage 5 marketisation could be discursively encouraged in a more positive register, albeit with attendant, even existential, risks for the weakest performers. Stage 5 also creates a regulatory framework designed to expand the number of HE providers, thus expanding the range of choices for applicants and potentially lowering average fees.

4.3. CONCLUSION

From the preceding analysis, it becomes clear that the varying stages of marketisation have been based on discourses which are employed contingently and in response to factors often well beyond those within the gift of any government. Some policy discourses have fallen into abeyance, no longer required or fit for purpose, while some have been reimagined or put to other uses. The notion of quality, for example, has shifted discursively from an absolute definitive marker to a scaled indicator in order to actuate a market distribution of institutions and programmes of study differentiated by levels of quality. Elsewhere in the preceding discourses, notions of efficiency, affordability and accountability are employed in a different register in later stages than previously, reflecting the shifting burden of costs from the state to the individual provider or graduate. However, even this is partly chimerical because the huge rise in potential graduate debt since the 2010 fee rise actually obliges the state to intervene more than ever, given that the public purse underwrites unpaid loans. All the supposed benefits of shifting this burden – greater autonomy for institutions, more choice for applicants, expanding the system to meet national human capital – are either stymied by the necessary rigours of the specific English version of a neoliberal system or are subject as much as ever to the spectre of future unaffordability. So finely calibrated is the resultant financing of a system that simultaneously offers excellent higher professional careers and upward social mobility to the few and exhorts 'shopping around for best value' to the many, it is difficult to see how this serves the needs of any beyond the cloistered elite, ever more protected by the turmoil beyond the gates in a 'risk-based' future. Yet, all the various stages and phases of reform considered here, and earlier in history too if we think of the Robbins Report of 1963, were designed to challenge precisely this dystopian scenario.

Immediately after the passing of the HERA, the Conservative Party chose to fight, and almost lost, a General

Election in an effort to expand its majority. The opposition Labour Party campaigned largely on a manifesto commitment to abolish tuition fees completely and remove historic graduate debt. Soon after this chastening experience the Prime Minister Theresa May, MP, ordered a review of the financing of all post-2018 education (DfE, 2018), noting that:

> *The competitive market between universities which the system of variable tuition fees envisaged has simply not emerged [...] All but a handful of universities charge the maximum possible fees for undergraduate courses (Theresa May speech, 18 February 2018, Havergal, 2018).*

One of the review's questions in its call for evidence asks how the government could 'create a more dynamic market in price and provision between universities and across the post-18 education landscape' (DfE, 2018, 2). It was clear that the review would be limited in its scope, for example it should 'Place no cap on the number of students who can benefit from post-18 education' (DfE, 2018, 3) and consider;

> *How we can support a more dynamic market in provision, taking into account reforms already underway, whilst maintaining the financial sustainability of a world-class higher education and research sector (DfE, 2018, 2).*

This clause clearly signalled that excellence could not be threatened by any reduction in fee income for 'the world class' and 'research' part of the sector; yet, as May herself noted in the quote above, the competitive market system had (once again) failed to create the kind of price differential promised in a decade and half of marketisation discourse.

How, then, can government square the circle? The Russell Group in its submission to the Review made it clear that:

> *Introducing a system of differential fees based on cost of delivery, graduate or social return, would likely be problematic and could have negative consequences for students as well as for universities and for the broader role they play in the economy and society (Morgan, 2018).*

Note that a system of differential fees based on quality (as measured by the UCAS tariff of applicants) is missing from the Russell Group's list of problematics; unsurprising given that this has been the mission group's preference since at least the late 1990s.

What, then, are the key drivers of English marketisation policy over the last 30 years? Clearly the dozen official policy documents analysed in this book offer us an insight into the dominant policy discourses that frame our 'neoliberal HE system' in the form of the nine analytical themes. However, on examination it becomes clear that there are many 'external' factors behind those discourses, outwith the internal logic of any overarching grand neoliberal project. Reacting to global pressure to maximise our national human capital; uncontrolled expansion prior to and after the unification of the HE sector (1992 F&HE Act), which in turn led to the formation of defensive 'mission groups' (the Russell Group and 1994 Group) precisely to establish differentiation; and the gradual cross-party acceptance of the idea that students would have to pay something towards their tuition costs if the system were to be expanded.

Once again we are confronted with a disparity between what the state declared (diversity as a good thing, HEFCE, 2000) and what DfES policymakers were being lobbied to provide (variable tuition fees to create a differentiated marketplace) in the same period of the run-up to the 2003 White Paper; as we know, the Russell Group had been arguing for such 'top-up' fees since the Dearing Review six years earlier. The first appearance of domestic institutional league tables in 2005 were another external motive factor, driving the conception and rhetoric of applicant choice in an aspirational market that merely burnished the credentials of large research-intensive universities, featured in no state policy statement, and indeed preceded the appearance of state-sponsored measures such as the NSS, UNISTATS and the DLHE.

While the introduction of such mechanisms of competitive differentiation in Stages 2 and 3 of marketisation policy can be seen as a post hoc discursive rationale of reforms elite lobbyists desired, there are other external factors in play that were both surely unforeseen and unwelcome. The 2008 financial crash, for example, was purely a global phenomenon requiring a national response, as with the effects of rapid (and unplanned) expansion of places between the late 1980s and late 1990s. In both cases, a reform to the financing of HE was necessary; after 2010, so wedded were successive governments to the benefits of competitive differentiation as the only mechanism by which to lower the average tuition fee (to the affordability threshold of £7,500 per annum) that whole swathes of well-regarded HE institutions were obliged to be subjected to a regulatory regime menaced by the existential risk of market exit.

If this analysis gives us cause to reconsider the usefulness of neoliberalism as causal driver in the name of some 'grand plan' then it has been worth the endeavour. Neoliberalism may not have much analytical or explanatory power if reduced to a post hoc rationalisation – or demonisation – of a chaotic period of exponential marketisation; however, it is perhaps worth considering whether the reforms latterly introduced in England take the system beyond the constraining definition of neoliberalism outlined in the Introduction to this book. To recall, the working definition of the English neoliberal tuition-fee system appears in the middle ground between a freely privatised market and the continuation of state planning. It appears designed with several key characteristics in place: to encourage the individualised responsibilisation of risk in the labour market; to reduce public exposure to debt (because the state underwrites tuition fees and thus carries the risk of non-repayment), yet at the same time to ensure the system is responsive to labour market needs and the national economic imperative. It consists of some market incentives, but contained within a regulatory system to control the overall quality, size and shape of the sector. A neoliberal HE system is thus an alternative to a truly open market driven by an 'invisible hand' (Meek, 2000). From the outside, it manifests as a market contained by a system of policy levers operated by the state; internally, neoliberalism is manifested as the application of selected market incentives in order to shape preferences and outcomes, bounded by a single regulatory framework.

The preceding analysis suggests that the definition still holds, albeit the 2017 HERA regime did offer some prospects of a 'free' market effect breaking those system constraints. The TEF, as first envisaged, offered the potential for a new way of defining the notion of excellence in the relatively entrenched hierarchy of English institutions (Boliver, 2011). If institution more noted for their teaching than their research excellence could infiltrate the upper reaches of league tables, this could provide an alternative market signal for applicant consumers, including a price differential; however, later iterations of the TEF removed the price differential linkage and the introduction of the subject-level TEF rankings is likely to water down the overall institutional association with excellence. Conversely, the much-vaunted level regulatory playing field for all HE providers operated by the OfS has been compromised by allowing new challengers seeking DAP and often UT to enter the market with an advantage over established providers. Existing providers now face competition from new providers unhampered by the same regulations – the precise opposite of the avowed policy intention. These instances perhaps reiterate the wider argument of this book, that while there is a distinctive English-variant of neoliberalism at play, it is actually contingent and pliable rather than 'grand designed' and imposed from without. Rather it reflects largely what the dominant policy actors – such as the defenders of a research-intensive world-class elite set of universities and successive governments increasingly desperate to reduce average tuition fees and public spending – want it to reflect.

BIBLIOGRAPHY

Admissions to Higher Education Steering Group. (2004). *Fair admissions to higher education: Recommendations for good practice (Schwartz Report)*. London: Department for Education and Skills.

Adnett, N., McCaig, C., Bowers-Brown, T., & Slack, K. (2011). Achieving "transparency, consistency and fairness" in English HE admissions: Progress since Schwartz? *Higher Education Quarterly*, 65(1), 12–33.

Agasisti, T., & Catalano, G. (2006). Governance models of university systems – towards quasi-markets? Tendencies and perspectives: A European comparison. *Journal of Higher Education Policy and Management*, 28(3), 245–262.

Archer, L. (2003a). Social class and higher education. In L. Archer, M. Hutching, & A. Ross (Eds.), *Higher education and social class: Issues of exclusion and inclusion*. London: Routledge Falmer.

Archer, L. (2003b). The 'value' of higher education. In L. Archer, M. Hutchings, & A. Ross (Eds.), *Higher education and social class: Issues of exclusion and inclusion*. London: Routledge Falmer.

Archer, L. (2007). Diversity, equality and higher education: A critical reflection on the ab/uses of equity discourse within widening participation. *Teaching in Higher Education*, *12*(5–6), 635–653.

Barnett, C. (1986). *The audit of war: The illusion and reality of Britain as a great nation*. London: MacMillan.

Barr, N., & Crawford, I. (1997). Universities in the first division, *The Guardian*, 16 September 1997.

Boliver, V. (2011). Expansion, differentiation, and the persistence of social class inequalities in British higher education. *Higher Education*, *61*(3), 229–242.

Bowl, M., & Hughes, J. (2013). Discourses of 'fair access' in English higher education: What do institutional statements tell us about university stratification and market positioning? *Widening Participation and Lifelong Learning*, *15*(4), 7–25.

Bowl, M., McCaig, C., & Hughes, J. (Eds.). (2018). *Equality and differentiation in marketised higher education: A new level playing field?* Palgrave. Palgrave Studies in Excellence and Equity in Global Education.

Brown, R., & Carasso, H. (2014). *Everything for sale; the marketisation of UK higher education*. Abingdon: Routledge.

Browne, J. (2010). *Securing a sustainable future for higher education: An independent review of higher education funding and student finance*. London: DDBIS.

Cable, V the Right Honourable, Secretary of State for Business, Innovation and Skills. (2010). *A new era for universities*, speech to Parliament, 15 July 2010 https://www.gov.uk/government/speeches/a-new-era-for-universities

Callendar, C. (2009, May 19). *Institutional bursaries in England: Findings from the latest OFFA research*. Paper presented to the Nuffield Foundation Seminar Institutional Aid for Students in the UK and USA, London.

Chester, J., & Bekhradnia, B. (2008). *Financial support in English universities: The case for a national bursary scheme*. Oxford: Higher Education Policy Institute.

Coffield, F. (Ed.). (1998). *A national strategy for lifelong learning*. Department of Education, University of Newcastle.

Crequer, N. (1997). *Universities dig in over fees*, TES, 12 September 1997.

Croham Report. (1987). Review of the University Grants Committee (Chairman: Lord Croham), Cmnd. 81 (London, HMSO).

DBIS. (2009). *Higher ambitions: The future of universities in a knowledge economy. Executive Summary*, DBIS, November 2009.

DBIS (Department for Business, Innovation and Skills). (2011). *Higher education: Students at the heart of the system (Cm 8122)*. London: Stationery Office.

DBIS. (2015). *Fulfilling our potential: Teaching excellence, social mobility and student choice*. London: DBIS.

DBIS (Department for Business, Industry and Skills). (2016). *Success as a knowledge economy: Teaching excellence, social mobility and student choice*. London: DBIS.

DBIS. (2016a). *Success as a knowledge economy: Teaching excellence, social mobility and student choice*, White Paper Presented to Parliament by the Secretary of State for Business, Innovation and Skills by Command of Her Majesty, May 2016 Cm 9258 Crown Copyright 2016.

DBIS. (2016b). Higher education and research bill impact assessment. DBIS May 2016.

DfE. (2017). Universities rated in teaching excellence framework: UK university teaching quality recognised for the first time (Gov.UK). https://www.gov.uk/government/news/universities-rated-in-teaching-excellence-framework

Department of Education and Science. (1978). *Higher education into the 1990s*. London: HMSO.

Department of Education and Science. (1986). *Projections of demand for higher education in Great Britain 1986–2000*. DES 2904/8.

Department for Education (DfE). (2016). *Employment and earnings outcomes of higher education graduates: Experimental data from the longitudinal education outcomes (LEO) dataset*. SFR 36/2016. Retrieved from https://www.gov.uk/government/statistics/graduate-outcomes-longitudinal-education-outcomes-leo-data. Accessed on June 10, 2017.

DES. (1987). Secretary of State for Education and Science, *Higher Education: Meeting the Challenge*. London: Her Majesty's Stationary Office, 1987.

Dennison, J. D. (1989). Higher education policy in the United Kingdom – reformation or dissolution? *The Canadian Journal of Higher Education*, 19(1), 87–96.

DfE. (2018). Review of Post-18 Education and Funding: Terms of Reference. Crown Copyright, March 2018.

DfEE. (1997). *There must be no victims in a modern economy – Blunkett*. DfEE press notice 385/97.

DfES. (2003). *The Future of Higher Education*, Cm 5735, January 2003.

Dworkin, G. (1988). *The theory and practice of autonomy*. Cambridge: Cambridge University Press.

Evans, B. (1992). *The politics of the training market: From Manpower Services Commission to Training and Enterprise Councils*. London: Routledge.

Evans, G. R. (2015). Entrances and exits: Planning for failure in higher education provision in England. *Higher Education Review*, 48(1), 68–90. ISSN 0018-1609.

Evans, G. R. (2016). Alternative providers of higher education: What are the risks? *Higher Education Review*, 49(1), 5–25. ISSN 0018-1609.

Fairclough, N. (1993). Critical discourse analysis and the marketisation of public discourses: The universities. *Discourse and Society*, 4(2), 133–167.

Fairclough, I., & Fairclough, N. (2013). *Political discourse analysis: A method for advanced students*. London: Routledge.

Foucault, M. (1972). *The archaeology of knowledge*. London Tavistock.

Foucault, M. (1979). *Discipline and punish*. London Tavistock.

French, A., & O'Leary, M. (Eds.). (2017). *Teaching excellence in higher education: Challenges, changes and the teaching excellence framework*. Emerald Great Debates in Higher Education.

Fryer, R. (1997). *Learning for the 21st century*, Report of the National Advisory Group for Continuing Education and Lifelong Learning.

Gibbs, P., & Knapp, M. (2002). *Marketing further and higher education research: An educator's guide to promoting courses, departments and institutions*. London: Kogan Page.

Glennerster, H., & Hills, J. (Eds.). (1998). *The state of welfare: The economics of social spending*. Oxford: Oxford University Press. ISBN 0198775903.

Graham, C. (2013). Discourses of widening participation in the prospectus documents and websites of six English higher education institutions. *British Journal of Sociology of Education*, 34(1), 76–93.

Harrison, N. (2011). Have the changes introduced by the 2004 Higher Education Act made higher education admissions in England wider and fairer? *Journal of Education Policy*, 26(3), 449–468.

Havergal, C. (2018). May: leaving poorest with largest debts 'hampers widening access', *Times Higher Education*, 18 February 2018.

HEFCE. (1994). *Overview of Recent Developments in HE*. Bristol: HEFCE.

HEFCE. (1999). Widening participation in higher education: Funding decisions, Higher Education Funding Council for England (99/24), Bristol. Available at: www.hefce.ac.uk/pubs

HEFCE. (2000). *Diversity in higher education: HEFCE policy statement*. Bristol, HEFCE 2000/33.

HEFCE. (2009). Higher education in England: Achievements, challenges and prospects, Bristol, HEFCE 2009.

HEFCE. (2010). *Trends in young participation in higher education: Core results for England*, Issues Paper Bristol: HEFCE.

HEFCE. (2011). AAB+ Modelling. HEFCE 2011/20 Annexe D. Bristol: HEFCE.

HEFCE. (2013). *Trends in young participation in higher education: Core results for England*. Bristol: HEFCE.

Higher Education Quality Council. (1995). Choosing to change: Extending access, choice and mobility in higher education: Outcomes of the consultation. London: Higher Education Quality Council, 1995.

HM Government. (1992). *Further and Higher Education Act 1992*. London: HMSO.

HM Government. (2004). *Higher Education Act*. London: HMSO.

HM Government. (2017). *Higher Education and Research Act*. London: HMSO.

HM Treasury. (2013). *Autumn Statement 2013*. Command 8747. December 2013.

HMSO. (2017). *Higher Education and Research Act*. Norwich: The Stationery Office.

Hood, C. (1995). The "New Public Management" in the 1980s: Variations on a theme. *Accounting, Organisation and Society*, 20(U3), 93–109.

Huisman, J., Meek, L., & Wood, F. (2007). Institutional diversity in higher education: A cross-national and longitudinal analysis. *Higher Education Quarterly*, 61(4), 563–577.

Jarratt Report. (1985). *Report of the Steering Committee for Efficiency Studies in Universities* (Chairman: Sir Alex Jarratt), London, CVCP. http://www.educationengland.org.uk/documents/index.html

Kennedy, H. (1997). *Learning works*. Coventry: FEFC.

Knie, A., & Simon, D. (2018). Germany's excellence debate, *Times Higher Education*, 19 April 2018.

Kogan, M., & Kogan, D. (1983). *The attack on higher education*. London: Kogan Page.

Labour Force Survey 1996, cited in Labour Party. (1996). *Learn as you earn; Labour's plans for a skills revolution* (p. 8). London: The Labour Party.

Labour Party. (1996). *Lifelong learning*. The Labour Party.

Lynch, K. (2006). Neo-liberalism and marketisation: The implications for higher education. *European Educational Research Journal*, 5(1), 1–17.

Marginson, S. (2013). The impossibility of capitalist markets in higher education. *Journal of Education Policy*, 28(3), 353–370.

Matthews, D. (2013). Curnock Cook tells elite of leaner ABB catches ahead. *Times Higher Education*. 5 September 2013.

McCaig, C. (2000). *Preparing for Government: Education policymaking in the Labour Party*, PhD Thesis, University of Sheffield. Retrieved from http://etheses.whiterose.ac.uk/5657/

McCaig, C. (2011, February–April). "Trajectories of higher education system differentiation: Structural policymaking and the impact of tuition fees in England and Australia" in the Special Issue of the *Journal of Education and Work*: 'National Structural Higher Education Policy and Politics in Times of Globalization and their effects on social inequality', 24(1–2), 7–25.

McCaig, C. (2011a). Access agreements, widening participation and market positionality: Enabling student choice? In M. Molesworth, L. Nixon, & R. Scullion (Eds.),

The marketisation of higher education and the student as consumer. London: Routledge.

McCaig, C. (2011b). Trajectories of higher education system differentiation: Structural policymaking and the impact of tuition fees in England and Australia. *Journal of Education and Work*, 24(1–2), 7–25.

McCaig, C. (2015). The impact of the changing English higher education marketplace on widening participation and fair access: Evidence from a discourse analysis of access agreements. *Widening Participation and Lifelong Learning*, 17(1), 5–22.

McCaig, C. (2016). The retreat from widening participation? The National Scholarship Programme and new access agreements in English higher education. *Studies in Higher Education*, 41(2), 215–230.

McCaig, C. (2018a). English higher education: Widening participation and the historical context for system differentiation. In M. Bowl, C. McCaig, & J. Hughes (Eds.), *Equality and Differentiation in Marketised Higher Education: A New Level Playing Field?* Palgrave. Palgrave Studies in Excellence and Equity in Global Education.

McCaig, C. (2018b). System differentiation in England: The imposition of supply and demand. In M. Bowl, C. McCaig, & J. Hughes (Eds.), *Equality and Differentiation in Marketised Higher Education: A New Level Playing Field?* Palgrave. Palgrave Studies in Excellence and Equity in Global Education.

McCaig, C., & Adnett, N. (2009). English universities, additional fee income and access agreements: Their impact on widening participation and fair access. *British Journal of Education Studies*, 57(1), 18–36.

McCaig, C., Bowl, M., & Hughes, J. (2018). Conceptualising equality, equity and differentiation in marketised higher education: Fractures and fault-lines in the neoliberal imaginary. In M. Bowl, C. McCaig, & J. Hughes (Eds.), *Equality and Differentiation in Marketised Higher Education: A New Level Playing Field?* Palgrave. Palgrave Studies in Excellence and Equity in Global Education.

McCaig, C., & Taylor, C. A. (2017). The strange death of Number Controls in England: paradoxical adventures in higher education market making. *Studies in Higher Education*, 42(9), 1641–1654. (first published online on December 7, 2015). Retrieved from http://dx.doi.org/10.1080/03075079.2015.1113952

McGettigan, A. (2013). *The great university gamble: Money, markets and future of higher education*. London: Pluto Press.

McGettigan, A. (2018). Longitudinal Education Outcomes (LEO) data analysis: How to interpret LEO, Central Careers Hub https://www.centralcareershub.co.uk/longitudinal-education-outcomes-data/?mc_cid=0f10d1d8dc&mc_eid=13c6b46d2f&utm_source=Taskforce+Research+Mail&utm_campaign=ce6e207832-EMAIL_CAMPAIGN_2017_10_20&utm_medium=email&utm_term=0_2a7dc8d67d-ce6e207832-167506021. Accessed 7 May 2018.

Meek, V. L. (2000). Diversity and marketisation of higher education: Incompatible concepts? *Higher Education Policy*, 13, 23–39.

Mok, K. H. (1999). Education and the market place in Hong Kong and Mainland China'. Author(s): Ka-Ho Mok *Higher Education*, 37(2), 133–158.

Molesworth, M., Nixon, L., & Scullion, R. (2010). *The marketisation of UK higher education and the student as consumer*. London: Routledge.

Morgan, J. (2013). Winners emerge in tug-of-war for ABB students. *Times Higher Education*, 12 September 2013.

Morgan, J. (2018). English funding review warned over 'damaging' differential fees. *Times Higher Education*, 4 May 2018.

NCIHE. (1997). *Higher education in the learning society (The 'Dearing Report')*. London: HMSO.

Newman, S., & Jahdi, K. (2009). Marketisation of education: Marketing, rhetoric and reality. *Journal of Further and Higher Education*, 33(1), 1–11.

Office for Fair Access (OFFA). (2005). Strategic plan 2005-10. Bristol: OFFA.

Office for Fair Access. (2010). *What more can be done to widen access at selective universities?* OFFA. April 2010.

Office for Students. (2018). *Securing student success: Regulatory framework for higher education in England*, February 2018 OfS 2018.01. Presented to Parliament pursuant to section 75 of the Higher Education and Research Act 2017.

Paulsen, M., & St. John, E. (2002). Social class and college costs examining the financial nexus between college choice and persistence. *The Journal of Higher Education*, 73(2), 189–236.

QSC/CVCP. (1997). *A Special Digest Report: What they said to Dearing*, The Open University, 1997, Report of the Committee on Higher Education appointed by the Prime Minister. Volume 1: Report, *The Robbins Report*, 1963.

Reisman, D. (1997). *Crosland's future: Opportunity and outcome* (p. 85). Basingstoke: MacMillan Press.

Robertson, D. (1995). Universities and the public interest: Time to strike a new bargain? *Renewal, 3*(4), 38–51.

Sellar, S. (2013). Equity, markets and the politics of aspiration in Australian higher education. *Discourse: Studies in the Cultural Politics of Education, 34*(2), 245–258.

Shamir, R. (2008). The age of responsibilization: On market-embedded morality. *Economy and Society, 37*(1), 1–19. doi:10.1080/03085140701760833

Simon, B. (1991). *Education and the social order, 1940–1990*. London: Lawrence & Wishart.

Social Mobility Commission (SMC). (2009, January). *Report from the Independent Commission on Social Mobility*.

Social Mobility Commission. (2016). *State of the Nation Report*, November 2016 Gov.UK.

Sutton Trust. (2004). *The Missing 3000: State School Students Under-Represented at Leading Universities*. London: Sutton Trust.

Taylor, C., & McCaig, C. (2014). *Evaluating the impact of number controls, choice and competition: An analysis of the student profile and the student learning environment in the new higher education landscape*. York: Higher Education Academy.

The Review of the University Grants Committee. (Croham Report) (HMSO 1987).

The Robbins Report. (1963). *Higher education: Report of the Committee appointed by the Prime Minister under the*

Chairmanship of Lord Robbins. London: Her Majesty's Stationery Office.

Thompson, A. (1997). *No extra cash as Treasury grabs fees*, THES, 22 August 1997.

UCAS. (2013). *2013 Application Cycle: End of Cycle Report*. UCAS Analysis and Research. December 2013.

Varman, R., Saha, B., & Skålén, P. (2011). Market subjectivity and neoliberal governmentality in higher education. *Journal of Marketing Management, 27*, 11–12.

Walford, G. (1988). The privatisation of British higher education. *European Journal of Education, 23*(1/2), 47–64.

Wiener, M. J. (1981). *English culture and the decline of the industrial spirit, 1850–1980*. Cambridge: Cambridge University Press.

Willets, D. (2010). Speech by Minister for Higher Education David Willets, House of Commons, 3 November 2010.

WonkHE. (2018). Regulatory Framework 2.0 – What you need to know, Catherine Boyd, 28 February 2018. https://wonkhe.com/blogs/regulatory-framework-2-0-what-you-need-to-know/. Accessed 24 April 2018.

World Economic Forum and the International Institute for Management Development. (1995). *The 1995 World Competitiveness Report, 1995*.

INDEX

Academic capitalism, 12, 128
Academic freedom, 32, 120
Academic tenure, 32
Access and Participation Agreement, 60, 66, 104
Accreditation, 20, 39
Acts of Parliament, 3, 22, 25
Affordability, 159
Aimhigher, 75, 134, 139
Anti-competitiveness, 113
Applicant
  choice for, 157–158
  risks, 97–102
Applicant-as-consumer
  point of view of differentiation, 14
Apprenticeships, 97
Approved providers, 103–104
Architecture reform, 98
Association of University Teachers (AUT), 38, 42, 46, 132
Attendance, 98

Autonomy versus centralization, 127–129, 145–147

Baker, Kenneth, 26
Barber, Pace, 121
Barber, Sir Michael, 118–120
Basic fees, 58, 75
Block grants, 128
Blunkett, David, 44
Browne, Lord, 71, 75–76, 135
Browne Review, 7, 57, 75, 80, 92–93, 137
BTECs, 86

Caveat emptor, 107–112
'Celebration of diversity' stage, 6, 130–132
Centralisation, 27
  versus autonomy, 127–129, 145–147
Challenger providers, 96
Chief Executive Officers, 29
Choice, as new frontier, 81–85

Clarke, Charles, 59
Code of Governance, 104
Collusion, 114
Committee of Vice-Chancellors and Principals (CVCP), 28, 32, 46
Communication, 21
Compelling value, 108
Competition, 71–76
  choice-driven, 82
Competition and Markets Authority, 103–104
Competitive differentiation, 10–11, 58, 92–94, 111, 137–141
Conservative and Liberal Democrat Coalition Government, 73, 138
Conservative Party, 25, 27, 28, 30, 33, 35, 38, 130, 150, 159–160
Consumer choice, 80
Consumer protection, 112
Consumer recompense, 112
Continuing expansion, 41
Continuing provision of course, guarantee of, 111–112
Course closure, 110–111
Credit Accumulation and Transfer (CAT) system, 39, 111, 130
Critical discourse analysis (CDA), 21–22

Croham Report, 29, 30, 51, 77, 128
Crosland, Anthony, 34

Dearing, Sir Ron, 38, 39, 42, 45–47, 49
Dearing Committee, 39–40, 44
Dearing Report, 46, 54
Dearing Review, 7, 45, 130–132
Degree awarding powers (DAP), 79, 83–84, 103, 105–107, 133, 142, 164
Department for Education and Skills (DfES), 29, 89, 108, 161
Department of Business, Innovation and Skills (DBIS), 71, 75, 89, 91, 122, 140
Destination of Leavers in Higher Education (DLHE), 88, 89, 134, 162
Destination of Leavers survey, 74
Differentiation, 71–76, 90–91, 132–137
  without competition, 68–70
  competitive, 10–11, 58, 92–94, 111, 137–141
  horizontal, 70
  vertical, 70
  market-incentivised, 77–81

neoliberal, 12–23
Diversity, 11, 38–43, 60, 77, 90–91, 113
  into 2000s, 47–51
  'Diversity as good' stage, 25, 152–154
  'Diversity to differentiation' stage, 57–94, 132–137
  2003 White Paper, 58–59
  choice, as new frontier, 181–185
  differentiation without compensation, 68–70
  Higher Education Act of 2004, 58–59, 68–70
  market-incentivised differentiation, 77–81
  student number controls, 77–81
  student number controls, strange death of, 85–89
  variable tuition fees, 59–68
Dual pricing, 67
Dynamism, 119

Economic crisis of 2008, 73, 137, 162
Educational attainment, 14
Education Reform Act of 1988 (ERA), 32–33, 51, 52–53, 128, 129
Education Reform Bill 1987, 128
Efficiency, 43–45
  in public services, 147, 148
'Efficiency and accountability' stage, 6, 10, 17–18, 25, 27–28, 52–55, 127–131, 134, 144
  business case for, 28–34
European Year of Lifelong Learning, 44

Fair access, 139
Fair Admissions to Higher Education: Recommendations for Good Practice, 69
Fee cap, 104
Financial competence, 29
Financial sustainability, management and governance (FSMG), 103
Framework for Higher Education Qualifications (FHEQ), 103
Fryer, Bob, 44
Fulfilling our Potential: Teaching Excellence, Social Mobility and Student Choice, 109
Funding mode, 147, 149
Further and Higher Education Act of 1992 (F&HE), 26, 35–37, 51, 53, 127, 129, 146, 161

Further education colleges (FECs), 6, 8
Further Education Funding Council, 44
Future of Higher Education, The, 57, 77

German Excellence Initiative, 3
Government incentives, 14
Graduate Contribution Scheme, 65
Graduate outcomes, 89
Graduate premium, 116, 134, 144
Green Paper, 3, 22, 97–103, 112–118
  2015 Green Paper, 143
  Opening the Sector to New Providers, 102–103
  Teaching Excellence Framework, The, 99–100
Guardian, The, 70

HEFCW, 96
Hierarchical system, 70
Higher Ambitions: the future of Universities in a knowledge economy, 57, 71–72, 77, 135
Higher Education Academy (HEA), 85, 86–87
Higher Education Act of 2004, 7, 13, 46, 58–59, 67, 89, 90–91, 136, 146
  limitations of, 68–70
Higher Education and Research Act of 2017 (HERA), 1, 6, 12, 19, 20, 39, 42, 64, 83, 95–123, 141, 159, 163
Higher Education – A New Framework, 35–36
Higher Education Funding Council for England (HEFCE), 36–37, 47–51, 55, 61, 63, 72, 84, 96, 104, 117, 130, 161
  mission statement, 47
  student number control analysis, 86
Higher education institutions (HEIs), 7, 8, 66, 79, 96, 107, 129, 134–136, 146, 147, 151
Higher Education in the Learning Society, 38
Higher Education: Meeting the Challenge, 30
Higher Education Policy Institute, 104
Higher education providers (HEPs), 96, 103, 106, 110, 111, 118, 120, 141, 142, 144, 145
Higher Education Quality Agency, 39

Index

Higher Education Quality Commission (HEQC), 111
Higher-status institutions, 8
HM Revenue and Customs data, 108
HM Treasury, 9, 85, 89, 94, 95, 140
Horizontal differentiation, 70
House of Lords, 32
Human capital, 6, 10, 19, 27, 31, 41, 45, 51, 72, 131, 135, 151
 maximisation, 43–45

Income, new sources of, 150–151
Income-contingent repayment system, 60
Incumbency, 113
Individual return on investment, 147, 148
Inflexibility, 113
Informed choice about alternatives, 98
Innovation, 119
Institutional autonomy, 34, 37, 50, 111, 119, 120
Institutional failure, risk of, 95–96
 regulatory reform, 102–107

Jarrett Committee, 28–34, 51, 127, 128
Johnson, Jo, 117

Kennedy Report, 44
Key Information Sets, 15, 88, 138
Knowledge economy, 6

Labour Force Survey, 44
Labour Party, 35, 38–44, 54, 58, 60, 71, 73, 80, 130–134, 136, 154, 156, 160
 tuition fees and, 45–47
League table rankings, 57, 87, 98
Learning society, 41, 43–45
Learning Works, 44
Level playing field, 9
Lifelong learning, 43, 131
Lifelong Learning Network, 75, 139
Local Education Authorities, 35
Longitudinal Educational Outcomes (LEO) data, 15, 108, 109, 118, 142, 143
Long-term demand, 41

Mandelson, Lord, 72–75
Market-incentivised differentiation, 77–81
Marketisation
 neoliberal, 4, 12–16
 discourse, cumulative effect of, 5
 see also individual entries

Market positionality, 21, 42, 74, 134
Market reforms, 25–55
Market segmentation, 89
Market share, 16
May, Theresa, 160
McGettigan, Andrew, 108–109
Means-tested maintenance grants, 60
Micro-management, 78
Missing 3000, The, 8
Mission groups, 3, 4, 6, 42, 131, 161
Mode of delivery, 13
Mumbai Declaration on Lifelong Learning, 44

NATFHE, 46
National Advisory Group for Continuing Education and Lifelong Learning, 44
National Committee of Inquiry into Higher Education (NCIHE), 38
National Student Survey (NSS), 15, 88, 89, 117, 134, 162
National Union of Students, 38–39, 58
Neoliberal differentiation, 12–23
Neoliberalism, 2, 12, 32, 126, 162, 163
  in English HE context, definition of, 16–20
Neoliberal marketisation, 4, 12–16
New Public Management, 6, 51, 127, 130, 147, 150
New Public Management Theory, 27
Non-repayment, 163

Office for Fair Access (OFFA), 21, 22, 60, 67, 69, 75, 96, 134, 139
Office for Students (OfS), 1–2, 96, 104, 117–119, 142, 164
Office of the Independent Adjudicator (OIA), 103, 104, 117
OFSTED ratings, 96
OPEC crisis, 25
Opening the Sector to New Providers, 102–103
Opening up the market, 157–158
Ownership, 21

Part-time learning, 13
Peer-review system, 129
Pluralism, 39–40
Policy discourse analysis (PDA), 3, 4, 12
  approaches to, 20–23
Policy shift, 105, 113
Polytechnic and Colleges Funding Council (PCFC), 32, 33, 36

Polytechnic Founding
    Council, 128
Polytechnics, 26, 27, 129
  establishment of, 34–35
Price competition, 144
Price differential, 67
Price indicator, 71
Privatisation, 130
Producer capture,
    113–114
Public expenditure, 76,
    110
Public sector, 31

Quality, 154–155, 159
Quality assurance (QA),
    103
Quality Assurance Agency
    (QAA), 39, 96, 103,
    130, 132, 142
Quality of teaching, 99,
    144

Rationalisation of
    policies, 2
Reduction in student
    number, 81
Regional Development
    Agencies, 73, 136
Registered providers,
    103
Regulatory reform of
    institutional failure,
    102–107
Regulatory regime, 96
Repayment, 65–66, 76,
    138
Reputational risk, 11

Research Excellence
    Framework (REF), 19
Residual household
    incomes (RHI), 46
Resource Accounting
    Budget, 89
Responsibilisation, 21
Retrospection, 18
Return on investment, 89,
    134, 139, 143–144,
    147, 148
'Risk and exit' stage,
    95–123, 141–145
  applicants and students,
    97–102
  caveat emptor, 107–112
  discourse development,
    112–117
  institutional failure,
    95–96, 102–107
Risk-based quality system,
    117–120
Risk-based regulatory
    system, 20, 154
Robbins Report, 27, 34,
    37, 41, 159
Russell Group, 6, 42, 45,
    62, 86, 132, 136, 139,
    161

Schwartz Review, 69
Science, technology,
    engineering and
    mathematics (STEM),
    75, 87, 136
Small Business, Enterprise
    and Employment Act
    of 2015, 108

Social class deprivation, 14
Social justice, 19, 136
Social mobility, 14, 19, 80
Social Mobility Commission (SMC), 57
State
  expenditure, discontinuation of, 75
  role in discourse development, 115
  role in system-shaping, 72
Student number control (SNC), 8, 9, 14, 84, 138, 140
  and market-incentivised differentiation, 77–81
  regime, 78–79, 88, 89, 101
  strange death of, 85–89
Students
  risks, 97–102
  satisfaction, 89
Students at the Heart of the System, 7, 58, 66, 73, 76, 77–78, 88, 99
Subject discipline, 13
Success as a Knowledge Economy: Teaching Excellence, Social Mobility and Student Choice, 112–113
Supply and demand, 89
Sutton Trust, 8
Swinnerton-Dyer, Sir Peter, 31
System delivery, 34–35

Teaching Excellence Framework (TEF), 9–10, 11, 15, 19, 83, 103, 104, 113, 117, 119, 142–144, 163
  ratings, 20, 96
  submissions, 21, 22
Teaching Excellence Framework, The, 99–100
Teaching quality, 63
Tier 4 licence, 103
Times Higher Education, 11
Times Higher Education Supplement, 70
Transfer system, 112
Tuition fees, 2, 7, 11, 15, 16, 18, 38, 45–47, 75–76, 126, 134, 137, 155–156, 163
  variable, 59–68, 133, 162

UK Commission for Employment and Skills (UKCES), 72
UK Research and Innovation, 104
UNISTATS, 73, 133, 135, 162
University and College Application System (UCAS), 8, 10, 14, 15, 67, 71, 82, 87, 117, 120, 137, 138, 143, 145, 154, 161
  tariff differentiation, 96

tariff distribution, 76
tariff requirements, 74
University Funding Council (UFC), 30, 36, 127, 128
University Governing Council, 26
University Grants Committee (UGC), 28–30, 127
University of Sunderland, 109
University title (UT), 79, 103, 105–107, 133, 142, 164
Utility maximization, 115

Vertical differentiation, 70

White Paper, 3, 7, 8, 22, 25, 31, 79, 95, 97, 101, 112–118, 140
  2003 White Paper, 58–59, 69, 90–91, 133, 134, 136, 141, 144
  2009 White Paper, 91, 136
  2011 White Paper, 93, 108, 138, 144
  2016 White Paper, 142, 143
Future of Higher Education, The, 57
Higher Education – A New Framework, 35–36
Higher Education: Meeting the Challenge, 30
Higher Ambitions: the future of Universities in a knowledge economy, 57, 71–72, 77, 135
Students at the Heart of the System, 7, 58, 66, 73, 76, 77–78, 88, 99
Success as a Knowledge Economy: Teaching Excellence, Social Mobility and Student Choice, 112–113
Widening participation (WP) policy, 7, 14, 19, 37, 43, 46, 50, 60–62, 68, 87, 97, 101–102, 131, 134, 139, 143, 152–154
  discontinuation of state expenditure, 75
Willets, David, 79
Work-based learning, 13
World Competitiveness Report, 44–45
World Conference on Lifelong Learning, 44